NEIL MUNRO & IAN STONE

Winning Words: Craft, Deliver, Succeed

The Entrepreneur's Blueprint for Strategic Communication

Copyright © 2024 by Neil Munro & Ian Stone

©2024 by Neil Munro & Ian Stone. All rights reserved. No part of this publication may be reproduced, distributed, or transmitted in any form or by any means, including photocopying, recording, or other electronic or mechanical methods, without the prior written permission of the authors, except in the case of brief quotations embodied in critical reviews and certain other noncommercial uses permitted by copyright law.

The information provided in "Winning Words: Craft, Deliver, Succeed - The Entrepreneur's Blueprint for Strategic Communication" is for general informational purposes only. All information in the book is provided in good faith, however, the authors make no representation or warranty of any kind, express or implied, regarding the accuracy, adequacy, validity, reliability, availability, or completeness of any information in the book.

The authors do not guarantee the success of using the techniques described in this book and are not responsible for any financial losses or other damages incurred from such use. Neither Neil Munro nor Ian Stone shall be held liable for any indirect, consequential, or special damages arising out of or in any way related to the use of the book.

Readers should apply the information in this book at their own discretion and consider seeking professional advice where appropriate for their specific circumstances.

First edition

Contents

IMPORTANT - READ THIS FIRST	iv
INTRODUCTION	viii
MASTERING THE ART OF LISTENING	1
THE POWER OF YOUR VOICE	13
NON-VERBAL COMMUNICATION CUES	24
CRAFTING COMPELLING MESSAGES	35
DIGITAL COMMUNICATION DYNAMICS	46
FEEDBACK MECHANISMS	57
NEGOTIATION AND PERSUASION TECHNIQUES	68
CONFLICT RESOLUTION STRATEGIES	79
BUILDING CHARISMA AND INFLUENCE	90
CONTINUOUS IMPROVEMENT IN COMMUNICATION	101
EMBRACING YOUR COMMUNICATION JOURNEY	113

IMPORTANT - READ THIS FIRST

Hello, we're Neil Munro and Ian Stone, and we're grateful that you've chosen to pick up this book. As seasoned entrepreneurs, business owners, and innovators in strategic communication, we've spent over two decades mastering the skills and techniques essential for successful interaction in the world of business and beyond. Throughout our careers, managing teams, speaking to mass audiences, and building businesses from scratch, we've encountered countless misconceptions and frequently asked questions about the art of effective communication. These experiences have driven us to compile our insights and hard-earned lessons into this much-anticipated book, aimed at guiding you to transform your communicative approach and enhance your leadership skills.

Maybe you've tried implementing new communication strategies in the past, only to find them falling short in real-world business scenarios. You've attended seminars, read books, and invested in expensive training sessions that promised to revolutionise the way you connect with clients, colleagues, and teams. Yet, the gap between theory and practice seemed insurmountable, leaving you frustrated and sceptical about your next steps.

Perhaps you've also been disappointed by generic advice that feels recycled and irrelevant to the specific challenges of your industry. These cookie-cutter solutions not only waste your time and resources but often leave you even more confused about whom to trust in your quest to become a more effective communicator.

Or maybe you've tried crafting your own methods, improvising as you go, only to face inconsistent results. One day, your improvised tactics seem to work; the next, they fall flat, leaving you doubting your ability to influence and lead effectively.

And we get it—it's not fair.

The reality is, you're not alone. Many business owners and entrepreneurs are stuck using outdated techniques and oversimplified advice that fail to address the complexities of modern business communication.

That feeling of isolation, confusion, and exasperation is something that many of us have faced at some point in our careers. It's incredibly disheartening to see your hard work and efforts go unrewarded, especially when you know deep down how crucial mastering communication is for your success.

What many people don't realise is that the landscape of business communication is constantly evolving. To stay ahead, it's not enough to simply adopt the latest strategies—you must also have a deep understanding of the psychological underpinnings of human interaction.

With the rise of global networking and digital communication platforms, the stakes are higher than ever. The ability to articulate your vision clearly and persuade others is no longer just an advantage; it's an absolute necessity.

Yet, so many find themselves in a state of perpetual uncertainty, unsure whether their communication skills can hold up under varying circumstances or with diverse audiences. This fear of being unable to convey your ideas effectively or influence others can lead to missed opportunities and, in some cases, potential business failures.

The Communication Carousel

In the fast-paced world of business, where every meeting, email, and handshake can determine the outcome of your success, many entrepreneurs find themselves trapped in a relentless cycle. This cycle, which we refer to as the "Communication Carousel," encapsulates the frustration of striving to become an effective communicator. As we explore this cycle, you'll see how the seemingly promising steps you've taken in the past have often led you around in circles, without ever truly breaking free.

Misunderstanding

Perhaps you've felt that sting when your message doesn't land as intended. Your innovative ideas fall flat or are misunderstood by your audience, leaving you questioning your strategy. This is the starting point—the moment when the carousel begins its spin. The frustration builds as you wonder why your clear vision isn't being received as you'd hoped.

Overcorrection

Driven by the desire to be understood, you may switch tactics, adopting new communication tools or techniques that promise instant results. This overcorrection can lead to messages that seem inauthentic or overly sales-driven, potentially alienating your core audience. Instead of building bridges, you may inadvertently create barriers, pushing your stakeholders further away.

Doubt

With each misstep, doubt creeps in. You start to question not only your communication skills but also your broader business abilities. This erosion of confidence can seep into other areas, impacting your decision-making and leadership. As doubt takes hold, your natural communication style may suffer, making your interactions feel forced and your leadership less inspiring.

Isolation

Feeling increasingly isolated, you might start to withdraw, opting for minimal communication to avoid further mistakes. This isolation cuts you off from valuable feedback, creating a vacuum where only your fears and frustrations echo. Important relationships with clients, partners, and even your team may suffer, stifling opportunities for growth and collaboration.

False Summit

Eventually, a new tool or strategy appears, claiming to be the ultimate solution. Hopeful, you embrace it, believing that you've finally found the answer to your communication woes. For a moment, everything seems to improve, and you feel as though you've conquered your challenges. But without addressing the deeper issues, this solution proves to be just another false summit. Before long, the familiar frustrations return, and you find yourself back at the start, ready for another spin on the carousel.

It's clear that something needs to change if you are to break free and become a truly successful communicator, free from the ongoing pain and frustration.

That's why we're thrilled you're reading this book. As you turn the pages, you'll discover the insights and practical strategies you've been searching for. Our aim is to equip you with the tools to finally overcome the Communication Carousel and elevate your communication skills to a level that drives real results in your business and beyond.

INTRODUCTION

Imagine, for a moment, you're at the helm of a thriving enterprise. Your product or service is innovative, your team is motivated, and your potential seems boundless. But there's a catch: if you cannot communicate your vision effectively, your brilliant ideas might never see the light of day. The art of communication, often overlooked, is the linchpin in the machinery of successful entrepreneurship.

In the bustling world of business, where every second counts and competition is fierce, becoming a masterful communicator can set you apart from the crowd. It's not just about conveying information; it's about inspiring action, persuading stakeholders, and building relationships that propel your business forward. This isn't just about talking the talk but ensuring your words lead to tangible outcomes.

The Transformative Power of Strategic Communication

You might wonder why some entrepreneurs seem to effortlessly sway investors, enchant customers, and lead their teams with charisma. The secret lies not just in what they say but how they say it. Strategic communication is a powerful tool—it can make or break deals, forge or hinder partnerships, and ultimately dictate the trajectory of your business.

In the realm of entrepreneurship, every interaction counts. Whether it's negotiating a deal, pitching to investors, or engaging with your team, the effectiveness of your communication can drastically impact the outcome.

The nuances of tone, the clarity of your message, and the body language accompanying your words all combine to either elevate or diminish your message's power.

The Journey to Mastering Communication

Now, envision yourself not just participating in conversations but commanding them. Picture your messages resonating, your suggestions inspiring action, and your voice holding the room. This isn't a skill reserved for the gifted few; it's an art that can be learned, honed, and mastered.

This book will serve as your map on this journey. You will discover how to harness the power of listening—not just hearing words but understanding contexts and cues that go unsaid. You'll learn how to use your voice not as a mere tool but as an instrument of influence, how to craft messages that captivate and convince, and how to navigate the digital landscape where emojis and emails carry your brand's voice across the globe.

Real-Life Applications and Unmatched Growth

As you advance through each chapter, the strategies discussed will increasingly reflect scenarios you encounter daily. From handling heated negotiations with poise and confidence to resolving conflicts that could otherwise escalate into crises, the applications of effective communication are comprehensive and transformative.

MASTERING THE ART OF LISTENING

"Most people do not listen with the intent to understand; they listen with the intent to reply." – Stephen R. Covey

The Foundations of Listening

Listening might just be the most underrated skill in your entrepreneurial toolkit. Think about it: every interaction, every negotiation, every piece of feedback hinges not just on what you say, but on how well you can tune into the other person. Getting this right can make the difference between a deal and a no-deal, a loyal customer and a lost one. So, let's break down the essentials of building a strong foundation in listening.

Active Listening Techniques

Active listening is not just about hearing the words; it's about fully engaging with the speaker. Imagine you're in a pitch meeting. Every nuance in the investor's tone, their body language, and their choice of words can give you clues about how to steer the conversation. Here's how you can master this skill:

1. **Give Your Full Attention:** This might seem obvious, but in a world where multi-tasking has become the norm, giving your full attention is a rare commodity. Put away your phone, turn off your laptop screen, and focus solely on the person speaking. Your undivided attention not only helps you absorb information better but also shows respect to the speaker, which can significantly enhance the relationship.

2. **Use Verbal and Non-Verbal Signals:** Nod occasionally, maintain eye contact, and use small verbal affirmations like "I see" or "Go on." These signals reassure the speaker that you are engaged and encourage them to continue.

3. **Paraphrase and Summarise:** Every now and then, repeat back what you've heard in your own words. This not only confirms that you are understanding correctly but also helps clarify any points that might have been ambiguous.

4. **Ask Clarifying Questions:** When there's a pause, ask questions that encourage deeper explanation or reflection. Questions like "What do you mean when you say...?" or "Can you tell me more about...?" show that you are interested and actively processing what's being discussed.

Remember, active listening is not about waiting for your turn to speak. It's about understanding the other person as completely as possible.

Barriers to Effective Listening

Despite your best intentions, several barriers can hamper your ability to listen effectively. Recognising and overcoming these can dramatically improve your communications:

1. **Prejudgements:** Entering a conversation with preconceived notions or judgments can colour your interpretation of what's being said. Try to approach discussions with an open mind, ready to receive new viewpoints.

2. **Distractions:** Physical distractions like noise or a buzzing phone, and psychological distractions like stress or personal problems, can make it difficult to focus. Strive to minimise these as much as possible when it's time to listen.

3. **Interrupting:** Cutting someone off not only stops them from sharing their full thought but also signals that you value your own words over theirs. Practice patience and let the conversation flow naturally without interjections.

4. **Over-preparing Your Response:** If you spend more time thinking about what you'll say next rather than listening to what's being said, you're likely to

miss key points. Stay present in the moment.

By being aware of these barriers and actively working to reduce their impact, you set the stage for more meaningful and productive conversations.

Empathy in Communication

At the heart of all effective listening is empathy. This is your ability to put yourself in someone else's shoes, to understand not just their words, but the emotions and motivations behind those words.

1. **Recognise Emotions:** Pay attention to the speaker's body language and tone. These can give you insights into their emotional state. Is their speech fast and choppy, perhaps indicating nervousness or excitement? Are their arms crossed in a defensive posture?

2. **Reflect Feelings:** Sometimes, it's helpful to acknowledge the emotions you detect. Phrases like, "It sounds like you're really passionate about this," or "I can see this is really frustrating for you," validate the speaker's feelings and encourage further openness.

3. Be Genuinely Curious: Approach each conversation with a desire to learn more about the person and their perspective. Empathy grows when you genuinely care about understanding others.

Incorporating empathy into your listening practices not only enriches your understanding but can also deepen your business relationships, making interactions more satisfying for all parties involved.

As you continue to develop your listening skills, remember that this is not just about improving how you absorb information, but also about fostering stronger, more respectful, and collaborative relationships. Whether with clients, colleagues, or potential investors, mastering the art of listening sets a strong foundation for your ongoing entrepreneurial success.

Listening in Different Contexts

Listening in Negotiations

Imagine you're sitting across the table from a potential business partner. The stakes are high, and each word could tip the balance of the deal. Here, listening becomes not just a skill but your best ally. In negotiations, effective listening enables you to understand the underlying interests behind what is being said, helping you to respond more strategically.

Start by focusing entirely on the speaker. This means putting aside your phone, shutting down your inner monologue, and ignoring distractions. Remember, good negotiators listen much more than they talk. They use their listening time to pick up on the other party's tone, pace, and choice of words, all of which offer insights into their current state of mind and ultimate desires.

One effective technique is to practise 'echoing'. This is where you repeat back what you've just heard in your own words. It shows that you are paying attention and also clarifies any points of misunderstanding. For instance, if your counterpart says, "We're looking for a long-term commitment," you might respond, "It sounds like stability is a key concern for you?"

Additionally, pay attention to what is not being said — the pauses and silences can also communicate volumes. These gaps often reveal uncertainty or points where the other party is expecting you to fill in the blanks. By being attuned to these subtleties, you can better navigate the negotiation to a favourable outcome.

Listening to Customer Feedback

As an entrepreneur, you know that your customers are your most valuable critics. Their feedback, whether it's praise or criticism, is integral in shaping your product or service to better meet their needs. However, truly listening to this feedback, especially when it's not wholly positive, can be challenging yet incredibly rewarding.

Start by creating multiple channels for feedback. This could be through direct emails, social media interactions, or feedback forms on your website. The key here is accessibility; make it as easy as possible for customers to communicate with you.

When you receive feedback, approach it with an open mind. Resist the urge to defend your product or service immediately. Instead, read through or listen to the feedback multiple times, if necessary, to fully understand the customer's experience and viewpoint. Acknowledge the feedback received warmly, thanking the customer for it, regardless of its nature. This not only shows respect but also encourages a culture of open communication.

Analyse patterns in feedback to identify areas for improvement. If multiple customers are pointing out the same issue, it's a clear sign that something needs your attention. Use this information to drive changes in your business. Demonstrating that you not only listen but also act on feedback can significantly enhance customer loyalty and satisfaction.

Listening During Conflict

Conflict is inevitable in any business setting. But when handled poorly, it can lead to lasting damage to relationships and the organisation's culture. Listening, particularly in these instances, can be a powerful tool to de-escalate tension and foster a more productive dialogue.

Begin by adopting a non-defensive posture. Whether the conflict is with an employee, a partner, or a team, it's crucial to listen without planning your counter-argument in real-time. This helps in understanding the core issues and emotions involved without bias.

Practise 'reflective listening' during these moments. This involves listening to the speaker's message and then reflecting or paraphrasing what they've said to ensure understanding. For example, if a team member is upset about feeling overlooked for a project, you might say, "It sounds like you're feeling undervalued because you weren't included in the project. Is that right?" This not only validates the speaker's feelings but also opens up space for deeper exploration of the issue.

Remember, listening during conflict isn't about agreeing with the other person but understanding their perspective. This shift in focus from winning the argument to resolving the conflict can lead to more creative and cooperative solutions, ultimately benefiting the business.

By mastering listening in these varied contexts — from high-stakes negotiations and receiving customer feedback to managing workplace conflicts — you equip yourself with a versatile tool that can significantly enhance your effectiveness as an entrepreneur. Remember, in the world of strategic communication, sometimes the most powerful thing you can do is listen.

Advanced Listening Strategies

Reflective Listening

Think of reflective listening as holding up a mirror to the speaker's thoughts and emotions. It's about rephrasing or summarising what you've heard to confirm your understanding. It's not just about repeating their words; it's about capturing the essence of their message and emotions. You, as an entrepreneur, can use this to ensure that your communication is not just heard, but understood deeply.

Start by focusing on the speaker, giving them your full attention. This might mean putting aside your thoughts, your phone, or any other distractions. As they speak, listen not only to the words but also to the underlying feelings and perspectives. Are they anxious, excited, concerned? Understanding these subtleties can significantly enhance the interaction and your business relationships.

When it's your turn to respond, reflect their message back to them. For example, if a team member says, "I'm overwhelmed with the project timeline," you might respond, "It sounds like you're feeling pressured by the current deadlines." This shows that you're not only listening but also empathising with their situation.

Reflective listening also involves asking questions to clarify your understanding further. Ensure these questions are open-ended to encourage a deeper discussion. Questions like "What aspect of the project do you find most challenging?" can open up a more fruitful conversation than simply advising or giving your opinion.

In practice, this method can prevent misunderstandings, build trust, and encourage a more open dialogue. When people feel heard, they are more likely to share their innovative ideas or voice concerns that could be vital to the success of your business.

Critical Listening Skills

While reflective listening focuses on empathy and understanding, critical listening sharpens your ability to analyse and evaluate the information being shared. This skill is crucial when you need to make decisions based on complex information, such as during strategic meetings or when receiving reports.

Critical listening involves a deeper engagement with the content of the message. You need to assess the logic, the arguments, and the reliability of the information. This means being alert to potential biases or assumptions that could colour the information shared.

For instance, when a sales team presents a glowing report on a new product's market performance, as a critical listener, you should examine the data supporting their claims. Ask yourself: Are the figures comprehensive? What are the sources of this data? Are there alternative interpretations?

Moreover, critical listening requires you to be both sceptical and open-minded. You might think of it as being a detective in a conversation where your job is to uncover the truth. This doesn't mean you should distrust every piece of information, but rather that you should seek to understand the full picture before forming your conclusions.

One effective technique is to mentally summarise the key points and reasoning behind them as you listen. This helps in retaining the critical information and also in identifying any gaps in the logic or areas where you need more explanation.

Remember, in business, the stakes are often high, and the information you base your decisions on needs to be accurate and reliable. Developing your critical listening skills can save you from costly mistakes and enhance your strategic decision-making.

Listening for Hidden Meanings

Sometimes, what's unsaid in a conversation can be as impactful as the words spoken. Listening for hidden meanings – or reading between the lines – involves picking up on the nuances, the tone of voice, and non-verbal cues like body language.

This skill is particularly valuable in negotiations or in gauging employee morale. For example, if an employee says they are "fine" but avoids eye contact and has a closed posture, they might be indicating discomfort or dissatisfaction. Recognising these cues can lead you to probe further or address potential issues before they escalate.

Developing this skill begins with an awareness of your own biases and preconceptions, which can affect how you interpret signals. It's important to remain neutral and focused on the speaker, without jumping to conclusions.

Practising this can start in less critical communications. Pay attention to casual conversations within your team or with business partners. Notice how their expressions or tone change with different topics. Over time, you'll start to notice patterns that can inform your understanding of more critical communications.

Listening for hidden meanings also requires a good degree of emotional intelligence. You need to be attuned to emotional shifts and the context of these shifts. Is there a particular topic that always seems to make your business partner uneasy? Is there a pattern in the way certain announcements are received by your staff?

By mastering this skill, you can anticipate problems, understand deeper motivations, and navigate business relationships more effectively. It allows you to connect with people on a level that goes beyond words, fostering a deeper trust and alignment with your business goals.

In conclusion, these advanced listening strategies are more than just techniques; they are essential tools that can dramatically improve how you interact and operate within your business environment. Whether it's ensuring that you have all the facts before making a decision, understanding the true sentiment behind a team member's words, or fostering a culture of open and effective communication, these skills are invaluable. They empower you not just to hear, but to truly listen and understand, paving the way for greater success in all your entrepreneurial ventures.

RECAP AND ACTION ITEMS

Congratulations on completing this deep dive into the pivotal skill of listening, a cornerstone for any successful entrepreneur. You've journeyed through understanding the foundational blocks, adapted your skills to various critical business contexts, and even stretched your capabilities into advanced listening strategies.

Firstly, remember that active listening isn't just about waiting for your turn to speak. It is about truly hearing what is being said. Practice the techniques discussed, such as nodding slightly or paraphrasing what others have said, to ensure you and your conversational partners are on the same page.

Secondly, be aware of the barriers that can hinder effective listening. Whether it's personal bias or noisy environments, recognising these hurdles can help you navigate towards clearer communication. Make a conscious effort to minimise distractions during important conversations — your smartphone doesn't always need to be within arm's reach!

Empathy in communication is your secret weapon. It allows you to connect on a human level and can be the bridge over troubled waters in difficult discussions. Try to put yourself in the shoes of others during your next chat; you might be surprised at the insight you gain.

Now, apply these listening skills in varied contexts. When negotiating, listen more than you speak; understanding the other party's needs can reveal the best path to a win-win outcome. Customer feedback is gold dust — don't just hear it, listen actively and use it to drive your business forward. During conflicts, keep your cool and focus on listening. Often, conflicts escalate because no one feels heard.

Moving to more sophisticated terrain, reflective and critical listening are your tools for not just understanding 'what' is being said, but 'why' it's being said. Practise these at team meetings or strategy sessions. Finally, tune your ear to pick up on hidden meanings — unspoken cues can sometimes tell you more than words.

Take action today. Choose one listening technique and focus on enhancing it this week. Whether it's maintaining better eye contact or noting non-verbal cues, small steps can lead to significant improvements in how you communicate and ultimately, how you lead.

THE POWER OF YOUR VOICE

"One cannot command attention by their silence." - Benjamin Disraeli

Vocal Mastery

Mastering the art of vocal delivery isn't just about sounding good; it's a strategic tool in your entrepreneurial arsenal. Whether you're pitching to investors, leading a team meeting, or engaging with customers, how you use your voice can significantly impact your message's effectiveness. Let's dive into the nuances of vocal mastery, focusing on tone and pitch control, rate of speech, and articulation and clarity. These elements can transform your verbal communications into compelling narratives that captivate and convince.

Tone and Pitch Control

First off, let's talk about tone and pitch. Your voice's tone can convey emotions and intentions, while your pitch can add dynamics and interest to your speech. A monotone voice might bore your audience, whereas an overly varied pitch might distract them. Striking the right balance is key.

Imagine you're discussing a new business opportunity. A lower pitch can portray confidence and seriousness, making your listeners take note of the significance. Conversely, a higher pitch might be useful when you want to express enthusiasm or urgency. However, too high can sometimes come across as anxious or lacking authority. It's about finding that sweet spot where your pitch reinforces your message, not undermines it.

Practising pitch control isn't just about varying your highs and lows; it's about using them strategically to enhance your key points. Try recording your pitches while speaking about different topics. Play them back to identify how your pitch changes with your emotions or the importance of what you're discussing. This self-awareness will allow you to start controlling it more consciously during conversations or presentations.

Rate of Speech

Now, let's shift gears to your rate of speech. Speaking too quickly can make you seem nervous or unprepared, while speaking too slowly might bore your audience or make you seem less enthusiastic. The trick is to modulate your speaking speed to match the content and context of your communication.

For instance, if you're explaining complex information, slowing down can help your audience absorb the material better. On the flip side, speeding up slightly can convey your excitement about a new idea or opportunity, which can be quite infectious.

A practical way to master this is through practising with different types of content. Read a piece of technical writing and try to explain it as if you're teaching someone with no background in the subject. Then, switch to something lighter, like a summary of a fun weekend, and notice how your speech rate changes. Being mindful of these changes and learning to control them will help you become a more effective communicator.

Articulation and Clarity

Lastly, we can't overlook articulation and clarity — they are the backbone of being understood. Mumbling or slurring words can quickly lose you credibility. Clear articulation, however, commands respect and ensures your message isn't just heard but understood.

Think about your articulation as the clarity of a photograph. Just as a high-definition photo allows you to see every detail vividly, precise articulation helps your listener grasp every word with ease. This clarity is particularly crucial when discussing nuanced topics or when speaking to an audience who may not share your first language.

To improve your articulation, start with tongue twisters. They can be a fun and effective way to practise enunciating clearly. Phrases like "She sells sea shells by the sea shore" or "Red lorry, yellow lorry" challenge you to focus on crisp sound delivery. Regular practice can significantly enhance the clarity of your speech in more formal settings.

Additionally, consider the volume at which you speak. Too soft, and you risk being tuned out; too loud, and you may seem aggressive. Aim for a volume that is audible and comfortable for your environment. This might mean speaking up in a large conference room or moderating your volume in a small meeting space.

By focusing on these three facets of vocal mastery — tone and pitch control, rate of speech, and articulation and clarity — you can elevate your speaking skills to match your entrepreneurial vision. Whether in a negotiation, a team briefing, or a client pitch, how you express yourself verbally can make the difference between being merely heard and being truly influential. Remember, your voice isn't just a sound; it's a powerful business tool. Use it wisely, and watch as doors begin to open in response to your newfound vocal prowess.

Expressing Authority and Confidence

When you step into a room or start a video call, the impact of your voice dictates how people perceive your authority and confidence. Mastering the art of confident vocal delivery can elevate your presence and influence. Let's dive into how you can use your voice to command presence, reduce stress, and strengthen your vocal confidence.

Using your voice to command presence

Commanding presence isn't just about being the loudest voice in the room. It's about how you use your voice to make people listen and respect your input. Think of your voice as your personal spotlight; wherever it points, people look.

Start with the basics: posture. Stand straight, shoulders back, head up. This isn't just good for your health—it directly enhances your ability to speak strongly and clearly. Air flows better through your lungs, your diaphragm moves freely, and your voice will naturally have more power and projection without straining.

Next, consider the power of the pause. In conversations, people often rush their words, afraid that silence shows a lack of knowledge. In reality, strategic pauses can emphasise your points and show that you're comfortable taking command of the conversation. A well-placed pause allows your words to resonate, giving your listeners a moment to absorb your ideas, and often drawing them in closer.

Varying your vocal pitch also plays a crucial role. A monotone voice can make even the most exciting news sound dull. By varying your pitch, you create interest and emphasis. That doesn't mean you need to fluctuate wildly but do try to convey your emotions through your pitch. Excitement, seriousness, urgency—all can be conveyed subtly through changes in pitch.

Lastly, be mindful of your volume. Speaking too softly can undermine your presence, making you seem unsure. Conversely, shouting can be perceived as aggressive. Aim for a strong, steady voice that projects confidence without overpowering your audience.

Techniques for stress reduction

Stress can strangle your vocal cords and make your voice squeaky or shaky. Reducing stress not only improves your health but also stabilises your voice, making you sound more assured and composed.

Breathing exercises are your first line of defence against stress. Before a big speech or meeting, take a few minutes to practise deep breathing. Inhale slowly through your nose, hold for a few seconds, and exhale slowly through your mouth. This not only calms your mind but also controls your heart rate and prepares your voice for speaking.

Visualisation is another powerful tool. Picture yourself succeeding in your upcoming speech or meeting. Imagine delivering your points flawlessly, receiving engaged nods and smiles from your audience. This mental rehearsal builds your confidence and reduces anxiety.

Don't underestimate the power of preparation. Know your material inside out. The more familiar you are with what you have to say, the less stress you will feel when delivering it. Confidence in your knowledge directly translates into confidence in your voice.

Lastly, regular physical activity can significantly reduce stress levels. Whether it's a morning run, yoga, or a quick workout session, keeping physically active helps manage stress, which in turn keeps your voice sounding authoritative and confident.

Vocal exercises for confidence

Vocal strength, like any muscle strength, comes from exercise. Practising specific vocal exercises can boost your confidence through improved control and capability.

Start with the basics: scales. Just like a singer, speaking through scales can help you control your pitch and strengthen your vocal cords. Start from a low note and gradually move up to your highest note, then back down. Repeat this several times, each time trying to keep your voice smooth and steady.

Tongue twisters are another excellent tool for articulation, which in turn builds confidence. Clear articulation ensures that every word is understood, which is crucial when you need to sound authoritative. Fast-paced and complex tongue twisters can help you improve your vocal agility.

Humming is a surprisingly effective vocal warm-up. It helps relax your voice and smooth out your vocal tone. Hum a simple tune, and focus on maintaining a steady, even sound. This not only warms up your voice but also calms your nerves.

Lastly, practice the art of projection. Stand in a large room or even outdoors and practise speaking to someone far away without shouting. Focus on making your voice reach out, filling the space with clear, resonant sound. This exercise will help you maintain a strong, confident tone that commands attention.

By incorporating these techniques into your daily routine, you can significantly enhance your vocal authority and confidence. Remember, your voice is a powerful tool in the entrepreneurial world—honing it can truly set you apart from the crowd.

Adapting Your Voice to Your Audience

Understanding audience demographics is crucial to the success of any entrepreneur. Imagine you're pitching your latest tech start-up idea in Silicon Valley versus presenting a new agricultural tool in rural Somerset. Both scenarios demand distinct styles and tones to resonate effectively with each audience. Your ability to modify your presentation based on who you're speaking to can make the difference between securing funding and walking away empty-handed.

Start by analysing the demographic characteristics of your audience. Age, education level, cultural background, and professional fields play significant roles in shaping how people receive and process information. For instance, a younger audience might appreciate a fast-paced, enthusiastic delivery peppered with contemporary references. In contrast, an older, more traditional group might value a slower, more deliberate speech pattern and a focus on reliability and experience.

Moreover, consider the setting. A formal investor meeting, a casual networking event, and a digital webinar each require different vocal styles. At an investor meeting, your tone might be more serious and formal, using technical jargon that shows your in-depth knowledge. Conversely, at a casual networking event, a lighter, more conversational tone can make you seem approachable, encouraging others to engage in conversation.

Tailoring messages to suit your audience is not just about swapping jeans for a suit or choosing PowerPoint over Prezi; it's also about aligning your message's core components to the interests and needs of your listeners. Begin by identifying the key benefits your product or service offers and match these to the specific concerns or desires of your audience.

If you're speaking to potential investors, focus on aspects like profitability, market potential, and return on investment. However, if your audience is potential users or customers, emphasize usability, cost-effectiveness, and how the product fits into their lifestyle. This alignment not only makes your speech more relevant but also increases the likelihood of your message resonating with the audience.

For instance, let's say you've developed a new piece of educational software. If you're addressing school administrators, highlight how your software can improve student outcomes and streamline lesson planning. However, if you're speaking to a group of teachers, focus on the software's ease of use, how it can save time, and enhance classroom engagement.

Modulating voice for engagement involves varying your pitch, tone, and pace to keep your audience engaged throughout your presentation. Monotone speeches can make even the most exciting topics seem dull and will quickly lose the audience's attention. On the other hand, a dynamic delivery can captivate and maintain audience engagement.

Practice varying your pitch to emphasize important points. A lower pitch can convey authority and seriousness, while a higher pitch might express enthusiasm and excitement. Similarly, adjusting the pace can impact how your message is received. A slower rate can help emphasize a point and allow the audience to absorb complex information, while a quicker pace can convey passion and urgency.

Don't forget the power of pauses. Strategic pauses can give your audience time to digest key points and anticipate what's coming next. They also provide you a moment to gather your thoughts and assess the audience's reaction to your message.

An effective exercise to improve your modulation is to read aloud a piece of text and consciously alter your pitch, pace, and volume throughout. Record this exercise and listen back to evaluate how changes in your vocal delivery affect the overall impact of the message. This practice can make you more aware of your vocal delivery choices and help you use them more effectively in live scenarios.

Remember, the goal of adapting your voice isn't to change who you are; it's about amplifying certain parts of your personality to better connect with your audience. Whether you're discussing the finer points of your latest innovation, networking at a conference, or leading a team meeting, how you say something can be just as important as what you say. By mastering the art of vocal adaptation, you not only ensure that your message is heard but that it resonates deeply with those listening, opening doors to new opportunities and paving the way for success.

RECAP AND ACTION ITEMS

So, you've just powered through some insightful strategies on mastering your vocal delivery. Let's crystallise that knowledge into actionable steps that will amplify your influence as an entrepreneur.

Master Your Vocal Mechanics: Start by recording your speech during a typical business interaction. Listen critically to the tone, pitch, rate of speech, and your articulation. Are you too monotone, too fast, or perhaps mumbling? Set a daily reminder to practice these elements. Use apps or tools that analyse speech patterns and provide feedback. It's like having a vocal coach in your pocket.

Command Presence Through Your Voice: Each morning, before you dive into your emails or your daily hustle, spend a few minutes on vocal exercises. Focus on breathing techniques that reduce stress and enhance vocal strength. A strong, relaxed voice exudes confidence and authority. Remember, your voice is not just a sound; it's your business's sound.

Engage With Your Audience: Tailoring your message doesn't just mean swapping a few words here and there; it involves a holistic understanding of who your audience is and what they care about. Before your next presentation or meeting, spend time researching your audience's demographics and interests. Adjust your vocal delivery to suit their preferences — perhaps softer and slower for a small group of investors, or more dynamic and varied for a large conference crowd.

Continuous Improvement: This isn't a one-off exercise. The most successful entrepreneurs are those who continuously refine their skills. Schedule regular check-ins on your vocal progress and adapt your training as you evolve.

Your voice is a powerful tool in the entrepreneurial toolbox. Use it wisely, and it will serve you well across boardrooms, phone calls, and global platforms. Start today, and let each word you speak be a step towards greater success.

NON-VERBAL COMMUNICATION CUES

> "The most important thing in communication is hearing what isn't said." - Peter Drucker

Body Language Basics

When you walk into any business meeting, your body is already chattering away before you've even uttered a hello. Mastering the art of body language can not only boost your own confidence but also influence how others perceive you in the entrepreneurial world. Let's break it down into posture and gestures, eye contact, and facial expressions to help you harness the full power of non-verbal communication.

NON-VERBAL COMMUNICATION CUES

Posture and Gestures

Think about the last time you saw someone slouching in a business meeting. Did they exude confidence? Probably not. Your posture is the cornerstone of your non-verbal arsenal, communicating your self-assurance and dynamic energy (or lack thereof).

Standing or sitting straight, with your shoulders back and head held high, doesn't just fire up your self-esteem; it broadcasts a signal of authority and openness to your audience. This is especially crucial when you're pitching to potential investors or leading a team meeting. A commanding posture invites respect and attention, crucial in any business setting.

Now, let's talk gestures. Have you ever watched a speaker who never varied their hand movements? It's like watching paint dry. Utilising hand gestures can help you emphasise points and keep your audience engaged. However, the trick is not to overdo it. Subtle gestures, such as showing your palms (which suggests honesty and sincerity) or using steepled fingers (often seen as a display of confidence), can effectively punctuate what you're saying.

But remember, while enthusiasm can enhance your message, too much can be overwhelming. Controlled gestures reflect controlled thinking, an attribute highly valued in business circles.

Eye Contact

Locking eyes isn't just for lovers; it's a powerful tool in business interactions. Maintaining good eye contact shows confidence and helps build trust with your audience. It tells them you're truthful and engaged.

However, there's a fine line between assertive and aggressive. The key is in the balance. In Western cultures, direct eye contact of about 60-70% of the conversation is appropriate. It shows you're interested but not confrontational. When you do look away, make it brief and try to keep your eyes up. Glancing down can suggest deception or a lack of confidence.

What about when you're dealing with larger groups? Let's say you're presenting to a room full of potential backers. Don't just fixate on a friendly face. Make sure to distribute your gaze across the room, making brief but meaningful eye contact with different individuals. This inclusion creates a connection with your audience, making each member feel acknowledged and engaged in what you're sharing.

Facial Expressions

Your face is a mirror of your emotions and thoughts, whether you're aware of it or not. A genuine smile, for instance, can be a powerful asset. It's universally understood and disarming, creating an environment of friendliness and openness. This is vital when you're fostering new business relationships or calming worried stakeholders.

But here's something fascinating: while smiles are great, not all smiles are created equal. A sincere smile engages the entire face, crinkling the eyes and moving the forehead. On the other hand, a fake smile tends to be a mouth-only affair. People subconsciously pick up on these cues, so a genuine smile can go a long way in establishing true connections.

Be mindful of other expressions too. Furrowing your brow or frequently frowning can give off vibes of worry or negativity, which might make others hesitant to approach you with ideas or issues. On the flip side, nodding while others speak or smiling at their comments can encourage more open communication and collaboration.

Your face doesn't just express how you feel; it can also influence how others feel about you. Controlling and being aware of your facial expressions can help steer conversations and negotiations favourably.

In the world of business, where every little advantage counts, understanding and mastering body language can significantly alter the dynamics of your interactions. Whether you're in a one-on-one meeting with a potential client or addressing your whole team, the way you hold yourself, your gaze, and your facial expressions play pivotal roles in the message you're conveying. Remember, in the realms of entrepreneurship, effective communication isn't just about what you say; it's also about how you say it—without actually saying it.

The Subtleties of Space and Touch

Understanding Personal Space

In the bustling arena of entrepreneurship, understanding the concept of personal space can be as critical as the business plan itself. Personal space, an invisible boundary surrounding us, varies significantly across different cultures and individual preferences. The general rule of thumb in a business context is to maintain a distance that is neither too invasive nor too distant, typically about an arm's length in most Western cultures.

However, as a business owner, your ability to read and respect these invisible boundaries goes a long way in building trust and rapport. For instance, if you notice someone stepping back or leaning away, you might be encroaching on their personal space. Conversely, if individuals seem to be leaning in, they might be comfortable with less space or more engaged in the interaction.

In a crowded networking event, space is at a premium, and your sensitivity to personal space can make or break potential business relationships. Always be observant of the cues others are giving about their comfort levels with proximity. If in doubt, it's safer to err on the side of caution and give more space rather than less.

Appropriate Use of Touch in Business

Touch is a powerful tool in communication, capable of conveying support, confidence, and sincerity. However, its use in a business setting must be navigated with care to avoid misunderstandings or discomfort. In a professional environment, appropriate touch typically includes handshakes, light pats on the back, or perhaps a guiding hand on the elbow. These gestures can reinforce a spoken message or serve as a greeting or farewell.

As an entrepreneur, mastering the art of the handshake is crucial. A firm, confident handshake can set the stage for a positive interaction, signalling both professionalism and openness. Meanwhile, remember that more intimate forms of touch, such as hugs or kisses on the cheek, are heavily influenced by cultural norms and individual preferences. These are generally best reserved for situations where you have a well-established relationship and are certain such gestures are welcome.

Incorporating touch, when done correctly, can enhance your communicative effectiveness. It can make you appear more personable and accessible, qualities that are invaluable in a leader. However, always be attentive to the other person's reactions and adapt your behaviour accordingly to ensure comfort and respect are maintained.

Cultural Differences in Non-Verbal Communication

As businesses become increasingly global, understanding the nuances of non-verbal communication across cultures has never been more important. What is considered polite or appropriate in one culture can be perceived as rude or intrusive in another. For instance, while maintaining eye contact might be seen as a sign of sincerity in many Western cultures, in some Asian cultures, prolonged eye contact can be seen as confrontational or disrespectful.

Similarly, the norms around personal space vary widely. In countries like the United States or the United Kingdom, people generally value a larger personal bubble. Contrast this with countries like Brazil or India, where closer proximity might be the norm, even in business settings. Knowing these differences can prevent unintentional offence and aid in smoother communication.

Furthermore, the use of touch in professional settings differs drastically across cultures. In some Middle Eastern countries, for example, touching between opposite genders in public, including handshakes, might be frowned upon. Meanwhile, in Mediterranean countries, gestures like kisses on the cheek as a form of greeting even in business contexts are not uncommon.

As an entrepreneur in the global market, make it your business to learn about these cultural specifics. This knowledge not only helps in avoiding faux pas but also demonstrates respect and thoughtfulness towards your international colleagues and partners. Tools such as cultural training workshops or even online resources can be invaluable in building this understanding.

Navigating the subtleties of space and touch in business requires a keen sense of observation, adaptability, and respect for diversity. By mastering these aspects of non-verbal communication, you enhance your ability to connect with others, build trust, and lead effectively across a variety of social and cultural contexts. Remember, in the world of business, sometimes it's not just what you say, but how you say it—or in this case, how close you stand and how you use touch—that communicates the loudest.

Interpreting Others' Non-Verbal Signals

Decoding body language is like having a superpower in the business world. It's about picking up on the subtleties that tell you what someone really thinks or feels, regardless of what they're saying. To master this skill, you need to pay attention to clusters of behaviours rather than isolated gestures.

Start with the basics: open versus closed body language. Open body language includes uncrossed arms and legs, relaxed hands, and a generally expansive posture that seems to welcome interaction. Closed body language, on the other hand, might involve crossed arms, clenched fists, or hunched shoulders, signalling discomfort or defensiveness. When you notice someone maintaining open body language in your conversations, it's often a green light—indicating comfort and receptiveness.

Beyond the open-closed dichotomy, consider mirroring—a phenomenon where one person subconsciously imitates the gestures, speech pattern, or attitude of another. If you observe someone mirroring your actions during a negotiation or meeting, it typically suggests rapport and a readiness to agree. Use this insight to steer the conversation towards consensus and mutual agreements.

However, interpreting body language isn't just about recognising comfort or agreement; it's also about detecting stress or insecurity. Look for signs like frequent touching of the face, throat, or mouth, which often indicate anxiety or uncertainty. Similarly, a person who is repeatedly checking their watch or phone might not just be busy—they could be disinterested or eager to escape the situation. Recognising these signals can help you adjust your approach, perhaps by clarifying your points or addressing concerns directly.

Non-verbal cues of deception are particularly crucial to understand. While no single gesture screams dishonesty, certain patterns can suggest that someone isn't being entirely truthful. For example, deceptive people often use barrier gestures, such as placing objects between themselves and others, to create a subconscious shield. They might also provide too much information, offering unnecessary details in an attempt to sound more convincing.

It's important to note that detecting deception based on non-verbal cues isn't foolproof. People are complex, and anxiety can sometimes mimic dishonesty. Therefore, it's vital to consider the context and to look for clusters of behaviours rather than jumping to conclusions based on a single sign.

Another telling sign is inconsistency between verbal and non-verbal communication. If someone says they're happy but displays a forced smile that doesn't reach their eyes (known as a Duchenne smile), their true feelings might be less positive. This disparity often reveals more than the controlled narrative that they choose to verbalise.

Using non-verbal cues for better negotiation leverages your understanding of these signals to influence outcomes favourably. When you enter a negotiation, your first goal should be to establish trust and rapport. You can do this by maintaining an open posture, using palms-up gestures, and nodding occasionally to show attentiveness and agreement.

During the negotiation, monitor the other party's body language closely. Shifts in their posture, such as leaning back suddenly or crossing their arms, can indicate discomfort with the terms being discussed. Recognise these moments as opportunities to pause and address concerns, or to recalibrate your propositions.

Effective negotiators also use timing and pacing to their advantage. Mirroring the speech rate and breathing patterns of your counterpart can create a subconscious sense of alignment, making them more receptive to your proposals. Additionally, strategic pauses can add weight to your statements and give others a moment to absorb and agree with your points.

Lastly, always be aware of your own signals. Consistency in your verbal and non-verbal communication enhances your credibility and persuasiveness. Ensure that your enthusiasm is conveyed not just through your words but also through your gestures and expressions. A genuine smile, steady eye contact, and confident stance can significantly strengthen your position.

In sum, mastering the art of interpreting non-verbal signals enhances not only your ability to understand others but also your capacity to influence and lead effectively. As you refine these skills, you'll find yourself navigating business interactions with greater ease and success, equipped with a deeper insight into the unspoken elements of communication.

RECAP AND ACTION ITEMS

You've just navigated through the intricate world of non-verbal communication cues, a vital skill that can significantly enhance your interactions in the business realm. Mastering this can elevate your entrepreneurial game, helping you connect better, convey your messages more effectively, and read the room like a pro.

Starting with the basics of body language, remember that your posture and gestures speak volumes before you even utter a word. Practise maintaining an open, confident posture and use gestures that are congruent with your words to reinforce your message. Next, never underestimate the power of eye contact and facial expressions. These are your tools for building trust and engagement. Try to maintain a balance where your eye contact is firm but not intimidating, and your facial expressions match the emotion or message you intend to convey.

Moving onto the subtleties of space and touch, be mindful of personal spaces and respect them. This awareness can prevent discomfort and help in creating a conducive environment for communication. In different cultural contexts, these norms can vary significantly, so take the time to learn about these differences especially if you're dealing with international clients or teams. The appropriate use of touch—like a firm handshake or a light pat on the back—can reinforce a connection or show affirmation, but always be guided by the context and the comfort level of others.

Lastly, interpreting others' non-verbal signals can give you a competitive edge in negotiations and in understanding underlying truths. Pay close attention to inconsistencies between what is being said and the body language displayed. This could be your clue to deception or uncertainty. Use your knowledge of non-verbal cues to steer negotiations in your favour, by responding appropriately to the signals you read.

Here are some practical steps to integrate these insights into your daily business interactions:1. **Practice Awareness:** Spend a week observing the non-verbal cues of others without trying to alter your behaviour. Note these observations down

2. **Experiment and Observe:** In the following week, consciously adjust your non-verbal cues during various interactions and observe the responses you get

3. **Seek Feedback:** Ask close colleagues or mentors to give feedback on your body language, particularly during important meetings or negotiations

4. **Cultural Learning:** If you're working in a multicultural environment, make an effort to learn about non-verbal communication norms from different cultures. Perhaps, start with the cultures most represented in your network

5. **Reflect and Adapt:** At the end of each day, reflect on your non-verbal interactions. Consider what went well and what could be improved. Adapt

based on your reflections.

By consciously practising these skills, you'll find yourself becoming a more effective communicator, poised to succeed in the complex world of entrepreneurship. Remember, the way you communicate non-verbally can just as powerfully impact your business outcomes as your words do.

CRAFTING COMPELLING MESSAGES

> "The single biggest problem in communication is the illusion that it has taken place." - George Bernard Shaw

The Structure of Persuasion

In the entrepreneurial world, your ability to persuade—whether investors, customers, or your own team—is often the linchpin of success. Mastery over the art of persuasion is not just a skill but a powerful tool in your communication arsenal. Let's break down this craft into its core components: elements of persuasive communication, building a logical argument, and the emotional appeal in persuasion. Understanding these facets can transform your interactions and elevate your impact.

Elements of Persuasive Communication

First off, persuasive communication is not about manipulation or deceit. It's about presenting your ideas in a way that resonates deeply and encourages others to share your vision. Here are a few critical elements to master:

1. **Credibility:** This is your foundation. If you're not viewed as credible, your message won't stick, no matter how compelling it might be. Build credibility through transparency, demonstrating expertise, and by being consistently reliable.

2. **Understanding Your Audience:** Tailor your message to the interests, needs, and emotions of your audience. Are they risk-averse or risk-takers? What are their values? What language do they speak in terms of their needs and desires? The more you know your audience, the better you can align your message to resonate with them.

3. **Clear Objectives:** Know what you want to achieve with your communication. Are you looking to inform, inspire, convince, or persuade to take action? Your

objective should shape the way you deliver your message.

4. **Engagement:** This involves not only grabbing but also maintaining interest. Use questions, anecdotes, startling statistics, or expressive imagery to make your communication compelling.

Each of these elements serves as a crucial cog in the machinery of persuasive communication. They ensure that your message is not only heard but felt and acted upon.

Building a Logical Argument

Now, let's stitch these elements into a logical framework. A cogent argument is structured and methodical. It makes your case irrefutable and your conclusion inevitable. Here's how to structure your argument:

1. **State Your Proposition:** Clearly define what you're arguing for. This is your thesis, your main point. Make it specific and unambiguous.

2. **Present Supporting Evidence:** This is where your preparation pays off. Use data, testimonials, case studies, or expert opinions to back up your proposition. Make sure your sources are credible and relevant.

3. **Explain Your Evidence:** Don't just throw data and expect it to stick. Explain how this evidence supports your proposition. Connect the dots for your audience.

4. **Address Counterarguments:** What objections might your audience have? Address these head-on. This not only shows that you've thought things through, but also that you respect your audience's intelligence and concerns.

5. **Summarise and Conclude**: Reinforce your main points and drive home the proposition. Leave your audience with no doubt about what you believe and

what you are asking of them.

The structure of your argument should flow as naturally as a conversation. Each point leads logically to the next, building momentum and pulling your audience along with you.

Emotional Appeal in Persuasion

While logic is critical, emotion is the secret sauce. We're emotional beings, and often, our decisions are driven by how we feel. Here's how you can weave emotional appeal into your persuasive efforts:

1. **Tell Stories:** Humans are wired for stories. They can stir emotions and plant ideas and values in a way that lists of data simply cannot. Use narratives to paint a vivid picture of the challenges, the journey, and the triumphs.

2. **Use Vivid Language:** Engage the senses with descriptive language. Paint a picture, craft a scene, and let your audience "experience" the message. When people feel actively involved, they are more engaged and more likely to be persuaded.

3. **Highlight Benefits, Not Features:** Connect your proposition to the emotional benefits for your audience. Don't just talk about what your product or service does (features), talk about how it makes life better (benefits). Does it bring peace of mind? Does it create joy? Does it alleviate pain or fear?

4. **Appeal to Shared Values:** Identify and tap into the values you share with your audience. Whether it's innovation, integrity, freedom, or community, speaking in a value-laden language strengthens emotional bonds and persuasive power.

Integrating emotional appeal effectively ensures that your message is not just understood but also felt. It makes your communication not just persuasive but also memorable.

By mastering these facets of persuasion—understanding the elements of persuasive communication, structuring a logical argument, and weaving in emotional appeal—you equip yourself with a potent set of skills. These skills will serve you across all areas of business, from pitching to potential investors to launching a new product line. As you continue refining these skills, remember that the art of persuasion is a journey, not a destination. Each interaction is an opportunity to learn, adapt, and improve.

Clarity and Conciseness

Avoiding Jargon

When you're deep in the trenches of your industry, it's easy to forget that not everyone speaks your language. Jargon – those industry-specific terms and acronyms you use daily – can be a major barrier to clear communication, especially when you're trying to reach out to new customers or investors who aren't as familiar with your field.

The first step to eliminating jargon is recognising it. Start by identifying any words or phrases that are specific to your industry. Ask yourself, would someone outside my industry understand this? If the answer is no, it's probably jargon.

Next, simplify. Replace complex terms with simple, everyday language. For instance, instead of saying "We're leveraging our core competencies to facilitate a paradigm shift in the market," try "We're using our key skills to change the market." You've conveyed the same message, but in a way that's accessible to everyone.

Remember, the goal is to be understood, not to impress with your vocabulary. When you communicate in plain language, you're more likely to engage your audience and convey your message effectively.

Simplifying Complex Information

As an entrepreneur, you often have to explain complex ideas, whether it's your business model, a new product, or financial data. The key to clarity here is simplification and structure.

First, break down the information into manageable parts. Think about the most important aspects of what you're trying to communicate and focus on those. Don't try to cover too much at once. If you're explaining your business model, for instance, you might break it down into its core components: what you sell, who you sell it to, and how you make money.

Use analogies and metaphors to make complex ideas relatable. For example, if your business involves blockchain technology, you could compare the blockchain to a ledger in a traditional accounting system. This helps bridge the gap between unfamiliar concepts and familiar ones, making your message easier to grasp.

Visual aids can also be incredibly powerful in simplifying complex information. A well-designed chart, graph, or infographic can convey what words alone cannot. They help your audience visualise data and understand trends and relationships at a glance.

Techniques for Clear Communication

Clear communication is not just about what you say, but how you say it. Here are some techniques to help you deliver your message clearly and concisely.

First, be direct. Start with your main point or the most important information. This is especially effective in written communications like emails or business proposals, where grabbing attention from the get-go is crucial. If you start with the most compelling information, you're more likely to keep your reader's interest.

Next, use active voice rather than passive voice. Active voice makes your sentences clearer and more dynamic. Compare "The meeting was led by John" with "John led the meeting." The second sentence is direct and easier to understand.

Keep your sentences and paragraphs short. Long, rambling sentences can confuse readers and dilute your message. Aim for an average of 15-20 words per sentence and 3-4 sentences per paragraph. This not only makes your writing easier to read but also helps maintain the reader's attention.

Finally, edit ruthlessly. After you've drafted your communication, go back and cut out any unnecessary words or phrases. Be brutal in your editing to ensure every word serves a purpose. This doesn't mean your message has to be dry; rather, it should be lean and to the point.

By focusing on these areas — avoiding jargon, simplifying complex information, and applying clear communication techniques — you can ensure that your messages are not just heard, but understood and acted upon. This clarity and conciseness are crucial in building trust and credibility with your audience, whether they are customers, investors, or your own team. Clear communication is the foundation upon which successful businesses are built.

Storytelling in Business

Elements of a Good Story

In the bustling world of business, where data and figures often dominate, the ancient art of storytelling might seem quaint, perhaps nostalgic. But it's precisely because of its deep-rooted prowess in human culture that storytelling remains an incredibly powerful tool for entrepreneurs like you.

Let's break down the core elements that can turn a simple narrative into a compelling business story.

Firstly, the **hero**. Every story needs one, and in the context of your business, this could be your product, your team, or even your customer. The hero is the focal point around which your story revolves. It's their challenges and triumphs that will capture the imagination of your audience.

Next, there's the **quest**. This is the journey your hero embarks on. In business storytelling, the quest often involves overcoming a challenge or solving a problem that mirrors the obstacles your target audience faces. This alignment not only keeps the story relevant but also heightens the emotional investment of your audience.

Then we have the **antagonist** or the challenge. No good story is complete without conflict. Whether it's a competitive market, a personal struggle, or a technological hurdle, your story should have a clear obstacle that the hero must navigate. This element not only adds suspense and intrigue but also sets the stage for demonstrating the value and effectiveness of your business or product.

Finally, the **resolution**. Your story should lead to a satisfying conclusion where the conflict is resolved in a way that showcases the benefits and values of your business. This not only leaves your audience feeling resolved but also ties back to your brand's promise, reinforcing trust and credibility.

Storytelling for Brand Building

Your brand isn't just a logo or an array of products; it's the complete narrative that surrounds your business. This narrative helps to shape how your audience feels about your brand, influencing everything from consumer behaviour to brand loyalty.

Incorporating storytelling into your branding can humanise your company, making it more relatable and engaging to your audience. Consider how Apple doesn't just sell computers and phones; they sell sleek, innovative design and cutting-edge technology wrapped in a story of revolutionising how we interact with technology. Your story could be about innovation, unrivalled customer service, or sustainability—whatever aligns with your brand values.

The narrative should be consistent across all platforms and materials, from your website to social media to packaging. Consistency helps to reinforce your story, making it familiar and recognisable to your audience. When your narrative resonates with people, they're more likely to remember your brand and choose it over competitors.

Moreover, storytelling can differentiate your brand in a crowded market. It's not just about what you sell but the stories you tell that can make your brand stand out. For instance, if two companies sell similar organic snacks, but one frames their products within a story of passion for health and environmental stewardship, that brand may attract and retain customers who are motivated by similar values.

Using Narratives to Inspire Action

The ultimate goal of using stories in your business communication is to inspire action, whether that's attracting investors, engaging customers, or motivating employees.

One effective technique is to craft stories that lead directly to calls-to-action. For example, if you're launching a new product, you might share a narrative about the development process, highlighting the challenges your team overcame and the breakthrough moments. This story could then culminate in an invitation for the audience to try the product themselves or to attend a launch event.

Similarly, customer success stories are potent tools for demonstrating the value of your offerings. By showing how real people have benefited from your products or services, you encourage potential customers to envision similar outcomes for themselves. This method not only illustrates the practical application of your product but also taps into the emotional response elicited by seeing others achieve success.

Lastly, consider the power of visual storytelling. In an age dominated by digital media, videos and infographics can convey your narrative in a dynamic and digestible format. Visuals can often communicate complex information more effectively than text alone and are more likely to be shared, extending the reach of your narrative.

By mastering these elements of storytelling, you not only enhance the way you communicate but transform how your brand is perceived in the marketplace. Remember, in the end, people may not recall every detail of what you said, but they will remember how your story made them feel. And in the world of business, those feelings are what drive loyalty and decision-making.

RECAP AND ACTION ITEMS

You've now equipped yourself with a robust toolkit to craft compelling messages that not only communicate your vision but also persuade and resonate with your audience. From understanding the structure of persuasion, enhancing clarity and conciseness, to mastering the art of storytelling in business, each segment you've explored is crucial in its own right and collectively, they are powerful.

Firstly, reflect on the elements of persuasive communication you've learnt about. Consider how you can integrate logical arguments and emotional appeals into your next pitch or presentation. Start by outlining the key points you need to communicate, then weave in supportive data and narratives that tap into the emotions of your audience.

Next, focus on clarity and conciseness in your communications. Challenge yourself to cut through the noise by avoiding jargon and simplifying complex information. This might involve reworking your current marketing materials or redefining your business proposals. Try using the techniques for clear communication to refine how you convey your business's unique value proposition.

Lastly, let's not underestimate the power of storytelling. Begin to craft stories that encapsulate your brand's ethos. Think about how these narratives can not only reflect your brand's identity but also inspire action and build stronger connections with your audience. Whether it's through your website, social media, or direct interactions with clients, use storytelling to enhance your brand's presence and influence.

As action steps, here are three tasks to implement what you've learned:

1. **Create a Persuasive Outline:** For your next important communication, draft an outline that includes logical arguments supported by data and emotional appeals. Use this to guide the creation of your full content.

2. **Revise for Clarity:** Take a piece of existing communication material and revise it for clarity and conciseness. Remove jargon and break down complex ideas into digestible, straightforward language.

3. **Narrative Building:** Develop a short story or anecdote that represents your brand or a key business lesson you've learned. Share this story in your next team meeting or include it in your next newsletter.

By actively applying these principles, you'll enhance your strategic communication skills, making your messages more impactful and memorable. Remember, the art of communication is a continuous journey of improvement and adaptation. Always be refining, always be engaging, and most importantly, always be authentic to your vision and values.

DIGITAL COMMUNICATION DYNAMICS

> "The single biggest problem in communication is the illusion that it has taken place." - George Bernard Shaw

Email Etiquette

In the digital age, mastering the art of email communication is more crucial than ever, especially for you, the savvy entrepreneur. Your emails can build bridges or burn them, open doors or close them, all with the click of a 'send' button. Let's delve into how you can harness the full potential of emails to propel your business forward.

Crafting Effective Subject Lines

Think of your email's subject line as the headline of a newspaper article. It should grab attention, yes, but it must also be clear and succinct, giving the reader a precise preview of what's inside. The subject line is your first, and often only, chance to make an impression. If you fail here, your email might never be opened.

Start with clarity and specificity. Instead of "Meeting," say "Proposal Meeting Thursday 1 PM – Request for Your Input!" This immediately tells your recipient what the email is about and why it's relevant to them.

Keep it short and sweet. Aim for no more than 50 characters. Most people skim their inboxes, and long subject lines get cut off, especially on mobile devices. Use actionable language that encourages the recipient to open the email. Words like 'update', 'invitation', 'request', or 'introduction' serve well because they imply a specific action or offer something of value.

Personalisation can significantly boost your open rates. Including the recipient's name or a reference to a recent interaction can make your email stand out in a crowded inbox. For instance, "John, your insights on our last call could enhance this project!" feels much more personal and relevant.

Tone and Formality in Emails

The tone of your email should strike a balance between professionalism and personal touch. This balance depends largely on your relationship with the recipient and the context of your message. A good rule of thumb is to start formal and relax your tone as your relationship develops.

Always consider cultural differences, especially if you're dealing with international clients or partners. What passes for a casual tone in one culture might be seen as unprofessional in another. When in doubt, err on the side of formality – it's easier to warm up a conversation than to walk back a perceived slight.

The use of emojis or slang should be approached with caution. While they can make your emails feel more relatable and less robotic, they might also undermine the professionalism of your message if used inappropriately. A winking face emoji may be perfect for a message to a colleague you know well, but it's not suitable for an email to a potential investor.

Empathy is key. Always read your emails from the recipient's perspective. How are they likely to interpret your tone? Are you being clear and respectful of their time and input? This empathetic approach not only enhances clarity but also helps build and maintain professional relationships.

Email Follow-Up Strategies

Following up is an art form that, when done correctly, can significantly increase your engagement rates without crossing into annoyance territory. The key is timing and relevancy. A well-timed follow-up shows you're attentive and proactive, but bombard someone too frequently, and you could see diminishing returns.

A general rule is to wait two to three business days to follow up on an initial email. This gives your recipient enough time to respond amidst a busy schedule without feeling rushed. If you haven't received a reply, your follow-up should gently remind the recipient of your previous correspondence, possibly adding new information or a call to action that wasn't in the original email. For example, "I wanted to follow up on my previous email about the XYZ project. I've attached some updated figures that might help us move forward."

Automate when necessary. Tools like CRM software can be used to schedule and track your follow-ups efficiently. This is particularly useful when managing multiple threads or when precise timing is crucial.

Knowing when to stop is as important as knowing when to follow up. If you've sent two follow-ups and still haven't received a response, it's usually time to pause and reassess the situation. The recipient might be busy, disinterested, or both. Further emails might only serve to irritate rather than engage them.

Each email is a touchpoint that can strengthen or weaken your business relationships. By mastering the craft of compelling subject lines, maintaining an appropriate tone, and following up effectively, you position yourself and your business as both professional and personable in the digital space. As you continue to interact via email, keep refining these skills. The more thoughtful your approach, the more strategic your communications will become, paving the way for lasting business growth.

Social Media Interaction

Engaging Your Audience

In the world of social media, engagement is the currency. As an entrepreneur, your ability to spark conversations and build relationships directly influences your brand's perception and growth. Let's dive into some tried-and-tested strategies to keep your followers not just interested but actively participating.

Firstly, understand your audience. This seems obvious, yet many businesses spray and pray generic content, hoping something will stick. Instead, invest time in understanding who your followers are, what they care about, and how they communicate. Tools like Google Analytics and social media insights provide a wealth of information about your audience's demographics, their behaviour, and when they are most active. Use this data to tailor your content.

Content is king but context is queen. What works on LinkedIn might not resonate on TikTok. Each platform has its own language and style. For LinkedIn, professional and insightful posts work well, often with a focus on industry trends or leadership insights. Instagram and TikTok, on the other hand, are more visual and informal, perfect for behind-the-scenes content, short tips, or visually appealing posts about your products or services.

Interaction is a two-way street. When your audience takes the time to comment on your posts, make sure you respond. This doesn't just keep the conversation going; it also shows that you value their input. Tools like Hootsuite or Buffer can help you keep track of interactions across different platforms so you can engage promptly.

Lastly, don't underestimate the power of video content. Live videos on Facebook, Instagram, or LinkedIn allow real-time engagement, which can significantly boost your visibility and interaction rates. Prepare, but also be ready to improvise and interact with live comments to make the session more engaging.

Managing Online Reputations

In the digital age, your online reputation can be your strongest asset or your biggest liability. A few negative reviews or comments can tarnish an image you've taken years to build. Managing your online reputation proactively is crucial.

Always monitor your social media channels. Tools like Mention or Google Alerts can help you keep tabs on what is being said about your brand online. Quick responses to negative comments or reviews can mitigate potential damage and show that your business values customer feedback and is committed to resolving issues.

Create a positive footprint. Regularly publish customer testimonials, success stories, and positive news about your business. This doesn't just counterbalance the occasional negative comment but also strengthens your brand's overall image.

Be transparent. If mistakes happen, address them openly on your social media channels. Apologising and showing how you're fixing the issue can turn a negative situation into a demonstration of your company's integrity and commitment to customer satisfaction.

However, not all negative feedback is bad. Constructive criticism can be invaluable. Show your audience that you're receptive to feedback by engaging with it constructively. This not only improves your services but also builds customer loyalty.

Leveraging Social Media for Networking

Social media isn't just for marketing or customer service—it's a powerful networking tool. It can connect you with influencers, peers, and potential business partners across the globe.

Firstly, identify the platforms where your desired connections are most active. LinkedIn is a natural choice for professional networking, but Twitter, Instagram, and even Facebook groups can be equally valuable depending on your industry.

Once you're on the right platform, don't just network for the sake of networking. Be strategic. Share content that is relevant to your industry and engage with content posted by your potential connections. Commenting on posts, sharing insightful articles, and participating in discussions can get you noticed.

Virtual introductions can go a long way. If a mutual contact is willing to introduce you, that's gold. However, a well-crafted direct message introducing yourself and explaining why you're reaching out can also be effective. Keep it concise and personalised. Generic messages are easy to ignore.

Lastly, remember that networking is about give and take. If you're looking to receive advice or favours, be prepared to offer something in return, whether it's your expertise, a platform to share their work, or another form of value.

Social media offers a dynamic platform for engaging with your audience, managing your brand's reputation, and expanding your professional network. By adopting a strategic approach to social media interaction, you can not only enhance your brand's presence but also create meaningful relationships that could propel your business to new heights. Remember, in the realm of social media, consistency is key. Keep your interactions frequent and your content fresh, and you'll set yourself up for success.

Virtual Meetings and Presentations

Tools for Effective Online Presentations

In the digital age, the ability to convey your message clearly and effectively in a virtual setting can be as crucial as the message itself. Choosing the right tools is the first step to ensuring your online presentations hit the mark every time. From PowerPoint to Prezi, numerous software options exist, but your choice should depend on your specific needs and the complexity of the information you wish to present.

Consider platforms like Zoom or Google Slides for straightforward, easy-to-set-up presentations. These tools are not only user-friendly but also come with features such as live polling and Q&A sessions, which can make your presentation more interactive. For more dynamic presentations, advanced tools like Adobe Connect or Prezi can provide more visually engaging and interactive elements.

Remember, the effectiveness of your presentation often hinges not just on the content but on how smoothly the technology operates. Prior to your presentation, always run a technical check to ensure software compatibility with all potential systems and that internet connectivity is stable. This not only helps in delivering a seamless experience but also positions you as a professional who values the audience's time and engagement.

Engaging Remote Audiences

Keeping a remote audience engaged during an online presentation poses unique challenges. Unlike in-person meetings, you can't rely on physical presence alone to command attention. Instead, engagement must be fostered through clear communication, interactive elements, and visually appealing content.

Start by setting the right tone from the outset. A friendly greeting and a brief overview of what the presentation will cover can help set expectations and pique interest. Use storytelling techniques to make your points more relatable and memorable. Real-life examples, particularly those that resonate with common entrepreneurial challenges, can be particularly effective.

Interactive elements such as polls, quizzes, or even simple Q&A sessions can transform your presentation from a monologue into a dialogue. These tools not only encourage participation but also provide you with immediate feedback on how well your message is being received.

Visual aids play a crucial role in keeping the audience engaged. Use high-quality images, infographics, or videos to break up text-heavy slides and help illustrate complex concepts. Be mindful of your slide design; cluttered or overly complex slides can be off-putting and may lead to disengagement.

Handling Technical Issues

Technical glitches are almost a rite of passage when it comes to virtual presentations. However, how you handle these issues can significantly impact your credibility and the overall effectiveness of your communication.

Firstly, always have a contingency plan. Before your presentation, familiarise yourself with the platform's troubleshooting options and have support contact numbers at hand should you need them. Inform your audience at the beginning of the session that should technical issues arise, you have a plan to address them, which can help manage expectations and reduce frustration.

Secondly, maintain your composure. Technical difficulties can be stressful, but staying calm and composed is key. If an issue arises, acknowledge it, apologise once if needed, and move to fix the issue without fuss. Your audience will appreciate your professionalism and focus.

Lastly, consider recording your presentation. This serves a dual purpose: it provides a backup should significant issues disrupt the live session, and it allows your audience to revisit the content at their convenience. Many platforms offer built-in recording functions, making this an easy addition to your virtual presentation setup.

By integrating these strategies into your approach, you not only enhance the effectiveness of your online presentations but also underline your adaptability and professionalism—qualities every successful entrepreneur should embody.

RECAP AND ACTION ITEMS

Navigating the digital landscape is no stroll in the park, but with the right approach, you can turn each interaction into an opportunity to advance your entrepreneurial journey. We've covered the essentials of email etiquette, social media interaction, and virtual meetings and presentations. Now, let's put these insights into action.

1. **Crafting Effective Email Subject Lines:** Start by reviewing your recent emails. Identify which subject lines worked and which didn't. Experiment with different styles—be concise, clear, and ensure the subject line reflects the email's content. Try A/B testing with different subject lines for the same email to see what resonates best with your recipients.

2. **Tone and Formality in Emails:** Audit your last week's worth of sent emails. Are you striking the right balance between professionalism and approachability? Adjust your tone based on the relationship and context. For formal communications, keep it professional without being overly stiff. For more familiar contacts, it's okay to be slightly informal but always keep it respectful.

3. **Email Follow-Up Strategies:** Implement a follow-up schedule using a digital calendar or task management tool. Don't let potential opportunities slip through due to lack of follow-up. Remember, persistence pays, but always be courteous in your reminders.

4. **Engaging Your Audience on Social Media:** Develop a content calendar that reflects the interests and needs of your audience. Use tools like social media analytics to gauge what types of posts generate the most engagement, and tailor your content strategy accordingly.

5. **Managing Online Reputations:** Regularly monitor what's being said about your brand online. Set up alerts for your business name and key products. Quickly address any negative feedback with professionalism, and amplify positive messages to reinforce your brand's positive image.

6. **Leveraging Social Media for Networking:** Identify industry leaders and potential business partners on social media platforms. Engage with their content thoughtfully and consistently to build relationships. Don't just sell; add value.

7. **Tools for Effective Online Presentations:** Invest in reliable tools and familiarise yourself with their features before your presentation. This preparation shows professionalism and respect for your audience's time.

8. **Engaging Remote Audiences:** Keep your presentations interactive. Use polls, Q&A sessions, and breakout rooms if applicable. Remember, engagement is a two-way street; encourage participation and feedback.

9. **Handling Technical Issues:** Always have a backup plan. Whether it's an additional device ready or alternative software options, being prepared means you can handle any hiccup with grace.

Remember, the digital world is ever-evolving, and so should your strategies. Regularly review and refine your approach to stay ahead in this dynamic environment. Let's harness the power of digital communication to propel your business forward. Go out there, connect, engage, and succeed!

FEEDBACK MECHANISMS

> "We all need people who will give us feedback. That's how we improve." - Bill Gates

Giving Constructive Feedback

When you're at the helm of a business, mastering the art of giving constructive feedback is not just important—it's indispensable. Feedback, when done right, can fortify your team, enhance performance, and foster an environment of continuous improvement. Let's unpack the essentials of giving effective feedback: from cheering on your team, tackling performance issues, to nurturing a culture of open dialogue.

Techniques for Positive Feedback

It's often said that the carrot is mightier than the stick, and in the realm of feedback, this holds particularly true. Positive feedback is a powerful motivator, yet it's not just about throwing around a generic 'good job' here and there. It's about being specific, timely, and genuine.

First off, specificity is key. Instead of vague compliments, pinpoint exactly what your team member has done well. Did they nail a client presentation, or perhaps their meticulous project management saved the day? Acknowledge these specific achievements. This not only boosts the morale of the individual but also sets a clear benchmark for excellence within your team.

Timing also plays a crucial role. Feedback is most impactful when given promptly. It ties the positive reinforcement directly to the action, reinforcing good habits and practices swiftly. So next time you see something praiseworthy, don't wait for the annual review—say it there and then.

Lastly, sincerity matters. People can sniff out insincerity from a mile away, which can render even the most well-intentioned feedback void. When you give praise, ensure it's heartfelt and reflects your genuine appreciation. This authenticity strengthens trust and respect between you and your team members, which is crucial for any thriving business relationship.

Addressing Performance Issues

Now, onto the trickier side of feedback—addressing performance issues. This can feel like navigating a minefield. Done incorrectly, it can lead to resentment or a drop in morale. However, approached correctly, it can lead to growth, better understanding, and improved performance.

Begin by ensuring that your feedback is always constructive rather than critical. Focus on the issue at hand, not the person. Use "I" statements to express how the situation affects the team and the business, and avoid blaming language which can lead to defensive reactions. For instance, saying "I've noticed that deadlines have been missed which impacts the team's workflow" is more effective than "You're always late on your submissions."

Clarity is your ally here. Be clear about what aspects of their performance are lacking and why they need to change. This should be coupled with actionable steps or solutions to help them improve. For example, if a team member struggles with time management, suggest specific tools or techniques and perhaps offer training sessions.

Remember, the ultimate goal is to guide your team member back on track, not to chastise them. Make sure they understand that you are there to support them and that their growth aligns with the company's success.

Encouraging Open Dialogue

The final piece of the feedback puzzle is fostering an environment where open dialogue is the norm, not the exception. This means creating a safe space where team members feel valued and heard, and where feedback is not a one-way street but a dynamic dialogue.

Start by being approachable. Let your team know that your door is always open and that you welcome their thoughts and feedback on all aspects of business operations. This doesn't mean you need to agree with everything they say, but it's important they feel heard.

Active encouragement is also crucial. Regularly ask for feedback on your leadership and management style. This not only sets a precedent but also models the behaviour you wish to see in your team. It shows you're committed to self-improvement and value their input, which can encourage them to engage in similar reflections and dialogues.

Lastly, recognise and reward open communication. When team members take the initiative to speak up about difficult issues or offer constructive feedback, acknowledge their efforts. This can be as simple as thanking them in the moment or more formal recognition in team meetings. This reinforces that open dialogue is appreciated and vital for the business's health and growth.

In essence, giving constructive feedback isn't just about ensuring your business runs smoothly—it's about creating a supportive culture that encourages continuous personal and professional development. By mastering these techniques, you not only enhance your team's performance but also drive your business towards greater success.

Receiving Feedback Gracefully

Tips for Active Listening

Imagine this: You're in the thick of a hectic week, sprinting from one meeting to another, when a team member asks for a moment to share some feedback. Your mind is elsewhere, already on the next item on your to-do list. But here's where the art of active listening becomes your secret weapon in the entrepreneurial arsenal.

Active listening is not merely hearing words; it's about truly understanding the message being conveyed. It begins with giving your full attention. That means putting aside your mobile phone, closing your laptop, and focusing on the person in front of you. Show that you're engaged by nodding or using other non-verbal cues and asking clarifying questions. For example, if an employee is explaining a difficulty they encountered, you might say, "So, what I'm hearing is that you need more support on project X. Is that correct?"

Moreover, summarise and reflect back what you've heard to ensure there's no miscommunication. This can be as simple as, "It sounds like you're suggesting we need to revisit our strategy on Y to improve outcomes. Do I have that right?" This not only shows that you are paying attention but also that you value their input.

Remember, active listening also involves reading between the lines. Sometimes, what's unsaid is just as important as the words spoken. Pay attention to body language and tone to get a full grasp of the feedback. This holistic approach will not only enhance the quality of the information received but also strengthen the relationship between you and your team.

Managing Defensive Reactions

Receiving feedback can sometimes feel like a jab to your ego, especially when it's not entirely positive. However, managing defensive reactions is crucial to use feedback constructively. First, recognise that feeling defensive is a natural, human response. Acknowledge these feelings privately, take a deep breath, and create a mental buffer to give yourself a moment to process the information objectively.

A useful tactic here is to maintain a mindset of growth. Shift from thinking, "This feedback is criticising me," to "This feedback is helping me grow." It's about learning, not losing. When feedback comes your way, try to detach yourself from the emotion of the moment and think strategically about the benefits of what you're being told. What can this feedback help you improve? How can it make your business stronger?

Another effective strategy is to ask questions. This serves two purposes: it helps clarify the feedback and also shows the giver that you are open and willing to engage. Questions like, "Can you give me an example?" or "What specific changes would you recommend?" transform a potentially defensive situation into a constructive dialogue.

Remember, the goal of feedback is improvement, not criticism. By managing defensive reactions, you turn potentially negative experiences into opportunities for personal and professional development.

Using Feedback for Personal Growth

As an entrepreneur, every piece of feedback is gold dust. It's an opportunity to refine your processes, enhance your products, or improve your interpersonal skills. To truly benefit, you need to actively incorporate feedback into your personal growth strategy.

Start by keeping a feedback journal. After each piece of feedback, jot down the key points, your initial reactions, and how you plan to address the issues raised. Periodically review this journal to assess your progress and identify patterns. Perhaps you're frequently commended for your innovative ideas but also often reminded to give clearer instructions to your team. Recognising such patterns helps you understand where your strengths lie and what areas need more attention.

Moreover, set specific, actionable goals based on the feedback. If you've been advised to enhance your communication skills, perhaps set a goal to attend a workshop or read a related book. Then, apply what you've learned in real-world scenarios and seek out feedback on your improvements to keep the cycle of growth moving.

Finally, don't forget to acknowledge and reward yourself for making changes based on feedback. Personal growth is a journey, not a destination. Celebrating small wins not only boosts your morale but also reinforces the behaviour changes that you're striving to make.

In the fast-paced world of entrepreneurship, feedback is a vital tool that fuels your personal and business growth. By mastering the art of receiving feedback gracefully—through active listening, managing defensive reactions, and using feedback for personal growth—you'll ensure that both you and your business are continuously evolving and adapting. This adaptability isn't just a nice-to-have; it's a necessity in the ever-changing business landscape, ensuring you stay relevant, responsive, and resilient.

Creating a Culture of Feedback

Feedback Systems in Business

In the realm of entrepreneurship, feedback isn't just a tool; it's an integral system crucial for continuous improvement and innovation. Establishing robust feedback systems within your business can dramatically enhance not only the performance but also the motivation levels of your team. It's about creating a feedback loop where information and insights flow efficiently from one node to another, fostering a culture of growth and adaptability.

Start by setting a structure that encompasses all levels of your organisation. This could mean regular one-on-ones, performance reviews, or even anonymous feedback channels that allow employees to express their thoughts without fear of backlash. Technology can be a powerful ally here. Consider platforms like Officevibe or Culture Amp, which facilitate continuous feedback and offer analytics to help you understand team dynamics better.

Moreover, it's crucial to align feedback with your business goals. When feedback is directly tied to strategic objectives, it becomes more actionable and relevant. For example, if customer satisfaction is a key goal, implement a feedback system that captures customers' perspectives immediately after a service interaction. This real-time feedback can be incredibly valuable and can be funnelled directly to the relevant departments for swift action.

Training Teams to Exchange Feedback

Training your team to give and receive feedback effectively is like upgrading the operating system of your business—it enhances every function. Start with workshops or training sessions that outline not just the importance of feedback but also the practical methodologies of delivering it constructively. Role-playing scenarios can be particularly effective here, helping to demystify the process and reduce anxiety around feedback exchanges.

It's also essential to train your team on emotional intelligence. When people understand and manage their own emotions and those of others, feedback becomes less about criticism and more about constructive conversation. Encourage your team to practice active listening, which is an invaluable skill in this context. It involves truly hearing what the other person is saying, processing it, and then responding thoughtfully. This can transform feedback sessions from dreaded interactions into opportunities for professional and personal growth.

Another useful tactic is to create a feedback charter—a set of guidelines or principles that your business abides by when it comes to feedback. This could cover aspects such as timeliness, specificity, and the use of positive language. Having such a charter in place not only sets clear expectations but also provides a consistent framework within which your team can operate.

Integrating Feedback into Business Processes

To truly embed feedback into the DNA of your company, integrate it into your daily business processes. This means making feedback a part of project cycles, client interactions, and even internal meetings. After every major project, for instance, have a debrief session that focuses on what went well and what could be improved next time. This not only helps in fine-tuning your operations but also ensures that your team is continually learning and evolving.

In customer-facing roles, integrate feedback mechanisms at every touchpoint. For instance, follow up a sale with a customer feedback survey that assesses their satisfaction and gathers insights on your product or service. Use this data not just to address individual customer issues, but to spot trends and patterns that could inform broader business improvements.

On the internal front, consider the integration of feedback into your technological infrastructure. CRM systems, for example, can be configured to prompt team members for feedback after completing interactions with clients or concluding projects. This ensures that feedback collection is systematic and not reliant on individuals remembering to do it.

Moreover, feedback should be a two-way street. Encourage senior leaders to seek feedback from junior staff. This not only sets a powerful example but also opens up channels for insightful perspectives that might otherwise go unheard. When leaders demonstrate openness to feedback, it reinforces a culture where every voice is valued, and every opinion matters, driving home the message that in your business, feedback is truly integrated into the fabric of everyday operations.

By implementing these strategies, you'll not only foster a culture of feedback but also create an environment where continuous improvement is part of the norm. Your business becomes a dynamic entity, capable of adapting quickly and efficiently to meet challenges and seize opportunities.

RECAP AND ACTION ITEMS

Congratulations on making it through the comprehensive exploration of Feedback Mechanisms. By now, you've equipped yourself with essential strategies not only for giving and receiving feedback but also for fostering an environment where feedback flourishes.

Firstly, remember the power of giving constructive feedback. It's not just about pointing out what needs improvement; it's about motivating and building confidence. Start by regularly recognising the positive achievements of your team. Make it a habit to provide specific, actionable insights rather than generic comments. When addressing performance issues, approach the conversation with a focus on solutions and support rather than criticism. Finally, encourage an open dialogue by asking questions and showing genuine interest in your team's ideas and concerns.

On the flip side, receiving feedback gracefully is just as crucial. Cultivate the art of active listening—really hear what's being said without rushing to defend or explain. When you find yourself feeling defensive, take a deep breath and remind yourself that feedback is a tool for your own growth. Use it wisely to refine your strategies and develop your entrepreneurial skills.

Lastly, creating a culture of feedback within your organisation can transform the way you operate. Implement systems that make giving and receiving feedback a regular part of the business cycle. Train your teams not only to exchange feedback constructively but to seek it proactively. Integrating feedback into your business processes ensures it becomes a driving force for continuous improvement.

ACTION STEPS:

1. **Start Small:** This week, focus on giving each team member at least one piece of positive feedback and one constructive comment. Observe how they respond and adjust your approach accordingly.

2. **Reflect and Journal**: After you receive feedback, take ten minutes to jot down your initial thoughts and feelings. Reflect on these notes after a few days to see them with fresh eyes and decide on actionable steps.

3. **Feedback Training Session:** Schedule a training session this month on effective feedback techniques. Use role-playing exercises to make the learning experience engaging and practical.

4. **Feedback Integration:** Review your current business processes to find where feedback loops could be integrated or improved. Set a goal to implement at least one change by the next quarter.

5. **Regular Check-ins:** Implement weekly or bi-weekly check-ins with your team focused solely on feedback—what's working, what isn't, and how can everyone improve.

Taking these steps will not only enhance your communication skills but also build a stronger, more resilient business. Remember, the goal is continuous improvement, both for you and your team. Keep pushing the boundaries, and let feedback be your guide to success.

NEGOTIATION AND PERSUASION TECHNIQUES

"The most important thing in communication is hearing what isn't said." - Peter Drucker

Preparing for Negotiations

Research and Preparation Strategies

Imagine you're gearing up for a big game. The field? The boardroom. The opponents? Your negotiation counterparts. Just like in sports, the key to winning in negotiations starts long before you actually step into the arena. It begins with rigorous research and preparation.

First, know your opponent. Dive deep into understanding the other party's background, their business model, and their needs. Use resources like their company website, news articles, financial reports, and industry analyses to gather as much information as you can. This isn't just about knowing their strengths and weaknesses—it's about anticipating their moves and being two steps ahead.

Next, turn the spotlight inward. Understand your own position thoroughly. What is your ultimate goal from this negotiation? What are your limits? What can you offer that might be of high value to the other party but of low cost to you? It's also crucial to assess the non-negotiables for your side. This clarity will allow you to negotiate from a position of strength, not just necessity.

Lastly, consider the context of the negotiation. What external factors might influence the outcome? This could be anything from economic conditions, market trends, to regulatory changes. Being aware of these factors can help you craft a more strategic approach that aligns with broader dynamics.

Setting Negotiation Goals

Setting clear, strategic goals before entering a negotiation is like setting the GPS before a road trip. It guides your path and keeps you focused, no matter the distractions or detours along the way.

Your goals should be SMART: Specific, Measurable, Achievable, Relevant, and Time-bound. For instance, rather than a vague objective like "get a good deal," aim for "achieve a 15% discount on the yearly supply contract within two weeks." This clarity not only sharpens your focus but also provides a benchmark against which you can measure your success.

When setting these goals, think beyond the immediate. Consider the broader impact of each goal on your business. How will this negotiation affect your long-term relationships? Does it align with your company's strategic objectives? Sometimes, a win in the immediate term might not be beneficial if it jeopardizes long-term goals.

Also, prepare for multiple scenarios. What if the negotiation takes an unexpected turn? Have pre-planned responses ready for different outcomes. This preparation ensures you remain in control, no matter the direction the discussion takes.

Understanding Negotiation Styles

Understanding different negotiation styles not only helps you tailor your approach but also enables you to respond effectively to the tactics employed by the other party. Typically, negotiation styles can be broadly categorised into five types: competitive, collaborative, accommodating, avoiding, and compromising.

1. **Competitive negotiators** are assertive and uncooperative. They aim to win at the other party's expense. If you're dealing with a competitive negotiator, be clear about your objectives and boundaries. Don't be pushed into a corner, and ensure you're ready with data to back up your positions.

2. **Collaborative negotiators** seek win-win outcomes, where both parties feel they have gained something of value. When facing a collaborative negotiator, emphasise mutual benefits. Be open and suggest multiple options that could work for both sides.

3. **Accommodating negotiators** are cooperative but unassertive. They often yield to others' demands. If you identify an accommodating style in your counterpart, appreciate their flexibility but also ensure you don't exploit it. Strike a balance that fosters goodwill and long-term relationships.

4. **Avoiding negotiators** are unassertive and uncooperative. They try to sidestep confrontation. In these situations, encourage open dialogue and try to make the negotiation environment more comfortable and less confrontational.

5. **Compromising negotiators** are moderately assertive and cooperative. They look for solutions that will at least partially satisfy everyone. With compromisers, it's beneficial to propose middle-ground solutions and be willing to make concessions that do not undermine your key goals.

By identifying the predominant negotiation style of your counterpart, you can adjust your strategies and communication accordingly. This doesn't mean manipulating; it means fostering an environment where both parties can reach a satisfactory agreement.

In conclusion, your preparation for any negotiation sets the tone for how the negotiation itself will unfold. By conducting thorough research, setting clear goals, and understanding both your own and your counterpart's negotiation style, you equip yourself with the tools needed to not just participate but excel in the negotiation process. This preparation ensures you enter every negotiation with confidence, poised for success.

During the Negotiation

Tactics for Persuasive Negotiation

Stepping into the arena of negotiation, your preparation now shifts into real-time strategy and action. Persuasive negotiation isn't just about pushing your agenda but aligning your goals with those of your counterpart. It's a dance of give and take, powered by tactical empathy and strategic influence.

Start with active listening. This is your power tool. By actively listening, you show respect and gain insight into the other party's needs, wants, and limitations. Remember, people are more willing to cooperate if they feel understood, not just heard. Use phrases like "If I understand you correctly..." or "It sounds like..." to reflect your understanding. This not only clarifies communication but also builds trust.

Next, deploy the power of mirroring. Mirroring involves repeating the last three or four words your counterpart has just said, in a questioning tone. It encourages them to elaborate and reveals deeper insights into their priorities and pressures. It's subtle yet profoundly effective in making the other person feel validated and more open to your proposals.

Questioning is your scalpel. Use open-ended questions to steer the conversation and uncover useful information. Questions like "How would that work in practice?" or "Can you help me understand why this is a priority?" open up the discussion, giving you more room to maneuver and adapt your strategies.

Frame your proposals in terms of the other party's gains. It's not just about what you want, but how what you want aligns with what they want. Articulate your points in a way that underscores mutual benefits, making it harder for them to say no without going against their own interests.

Finally, control the pace. Sometimes, slowing down can give you an edge. If negotiations are moving too fast, take a pause. This allows you to think and stops you from making precipitous concessions. A well-timed pause can also create a sense of anticipation and make the other side reconsider their stance or come up with a better offer.

Managing Concessions

Concessions are inevitable in negotiations, but they should be managed smartly to ensure you don't give away the farm. Think of each concession as a strategic tool, not a retreat. Your concessions should always aim to create value that can be leveraged later in the negotiation.

Begin by establishing your walk-away point—the absolute minimum outcome you're willing to accept. This clear boundary will guide you in managing concessions without slipping into disadvantageous compromises.

When you do make a concession, ensure it's conditional. Never give something for nothing. Instead, tag your concessions with "if... then..." statements. For example, "I can meet this price if you can commit to a longer contract." This not only protects your interests but also keeps the negotiation reciprocal.

It's also vital to prioritize your concessions. Start with minor ones that don't cost you much but can mean a lot to the other party. This builds goodwill and can make them more receptive to your later demands.

Another savvy tactic is to hold back on some concessions until the end of the negotiation. These can be used as final sweeteners to clinch the deal, presenting them as big wins for the other party even if they were always on the table.

Remember, the goal with concessions is not to keep score but to move the negotiation forward in a way that benefits you.

Handling Objections

Objections are not roadblocks but signposts that guide you through the negotiation. They provide insight into the other party's concerns and priorities and are opportunities to refine your approach and offer.

First, anticipate common objections and prepare your responses. This preparation shows the other party that you understand their concerns and are ahead in thinking through possible solutions.

When faced with an objection, resist the urge to counter it immediately. Instead, use the technique of 'Feel, Felt, Found.' Acknowledge their concern (Feel), show empathy by suggesting others have felt the same (Felt), and explain how a solution was found (Found). For example, "I understand why you might feel this is too much of an investment. Others have felt the same way initially, but they found that the ROI significantly outweighed the initial outlay."

Use objections to ask more questions. This can uncover underlying issues that, once addressed, can dissolve the objections. For instance, if the objection is about cost, explore what budget constraints they are facing or what aspects of your proposal offer them the most value.

Lastly, don't be defensive. Treat objections as a chance to deepen the dialogue and demonstrate the robustness of your proposal. Each resolved objection gets you closer to a mutually beneficial agreement.

By mastering these tactics during your negotiations, you position yourself not just as a competitor, but as a collaborator striving for a win-win scenario. This approach not only increases the likelihood of a successful deal but also sets a positive tone for potential future business engagements.

Closing and Beyond

Effective Closing Techniques

Closing a negotiation isn't just about getting a signature on the dotted line; it's about achieving a conclusion that everyone feels good about, ensuring that the deal is implemented smoothly and paves the way for future interactions.

As an entrepreneur, mastering this final phase is as crucial as the preparation and process.

Firstly, clarify all terms and ensure mutual understanding. It sounds obvious, but misunderstandings at this stage can unravel even the most meticulously negotiated agreements. Make it a habit to summarise the key points, reiterating each party's commitments, and clarifying any final queries they might have. This is not just about avoiding misinterpretations; it's also an opportunity to reinforce the relationship by demonstrating thoroughness and attention to detail.

Next, always be ready to sweeten the deal—not necessarily with major concessions, but with small enhancements or assurances that show your commitment to the relationship beyond the immediate transaction. This could be a faster delivery time, a follow-up service check, or a discount on future purchases. These gestures make the counterpart feel valued and can turn a straightforward transactional relationship into a loyal, ongoing partnership.

Remember, the way you close the negotiation sets the tone for the implementation of the agreement and subsequent interactions. A respectful and thoughtful close increases the likelihood of a smooth transition to contract fulfilment and lays a strong foundation for potential future deals.

Building Long-term Relationships

The negotiation table is where relationships are forged. Viewing negotiations as a one-off event is a common trap many entrepreneurs fall into. However, in the business world, today's competitors can be tomorrow's partners. The end of a negotiation is just the beginning of a business relationship.

Building long-term relationships starts with a mindset that values mutual success over individual winnings. When you negotiate, aim not just for a good deal but for a good relationship. Be a tough negotiator but a fair one. Ensure that the terms agreed upon are not just beneficial but also sustainable for all parties involved. This encourages trust and respect, which are the bedrock of any long-term business relationship.

Post-negotiation, make an effort to check in on the progress of the agreement. Is everything proceeding as planned? Are there any unexpected challenges? Proactive communication can prevent small issues from escalating into bigger problems and demonstrates your commitment to the relationship beyond the deal.

Additionally, keep your network active even when you're not looking to negotiate. Share useful information, connect your contacts with opportunities, or simply catch up over a coffee. These interactions keep the relationship warm, making it easier to initiate new negotiations or collaborations in the future.

Learning from Negotiation Experiences

Every negotiation, whether successful or not, offers invaluable lessons that can refine your approach and strategies for future deals. The key is to systematically capture and analyse these lessons.

Start by debriefing after each negotiation. What worked well? What didn't? Were there unexpected obstacles? How did you and your team handle pressure points? This reflection should not be a blame game but a constructive review to build on your strengths and identify areas for improvement.

Documenting these insights is vital. Maintain a negotiation journal or database where you and your team can record details of each negotiation process: the strategies used, the tactics that worked, the challenges faced, and the outcomes achieved. This record becomes a practical resource for future negotiations, offering real-world examples of what has been effective or ineffective.

Moreover, share these learnings with your team. If you're leading a business, fostering a culture of continuous improvement in negotiation skills across your organisation can drive collective success. Regular training sessions, workshops, or simply sharing lessons in team meetings can help embed best practices and prepare your team for future challenges.

Lastly, don't overlook external learning opportunities. Engage with other business owners, read up on new negotiation theories, participate in forums, or attend workshops and seminars. The world of negotiation is dynamic, and staying updated with the latest strategies and trends can provide you with a competitive edge.

By focusing on these three critical aspects—closing effectively, building lasting relationships, and learning continuously from your experiences—you'll not only enhance your immediate negotiation outcomes but also cultivate a reputation as a savvy, strategic negotiator who is a pleasure to do business with. This reputation will open doors to new opportunities and enable you to navigate the complexities of entrepreneurial ventures with greater ease and success.

RECAP AND ACTION ITEMS

Congratulations! You've just armed yourself with some of the most effective negotiation and persuasion techniques out there. Remember, negotiation isn't just a skill—it's an art that combines psychology, strategy, and timing to achieve the best possible outcomes.

Let's quickly recap what you've covered. You've prepped yourself by diving deep into research and preparation strategies, setting clear and achievable goals, and understanding different negotiation styles. This groundwork is crucial; it sets the stage for the negotiation dance.

During the negotiation phase, you've learnt to deploy tactics for persuasive negotiation, manage concessions adeptly, and handle objections smoothly. These skills are pivotal in keeping you in control of the negotiation process, ensuring you can steer conversations towards your desired outcome.

Finally, you've explored how to close deals effectively and foster long-term relationships. Remember, the end of a negotiation isn't just about getting a signature; it's about setting the stage for future opportunities. Learning from each negotiation experience is key to becoming a master negotiator.

Now, it's time to put these insights into action. Start by reviewing your upcoming negotiations and apply the preparation strategies you've learnt. Identify the negotiation style best suited for each scenario and set clear, strategic goals.

During your negotiations, stay alert and responsive. Use the tactics discussed to remain persuasive and in command. Don't shy away from managing concessions; it's often necessary to give a little to gain a lot. Be prepared for objections and handle them with the finesse of a seasoned negotiator.

After each negotiation, take the time to review what went well and what could be improved. Use these insights to refine your approach for next time. And don't forget to invest in the relationships you've built; they could be your biggest asset in future negotiations.

Negotiation is a journey, not a destination. With each conversation, you refine your skills, build confidence, and increase your chances of success. Keep pushing, keep negotiating, and most importantly, keep learning. The art of negotiation is constantly evolving, and so should you.

CONFLICT RESOLUTION STRATEGIES

"Peace is not absence of conflict, it is the ability to handle conflict by peaceful means." - Ronald Reagan

Understanding Conflict

Types of Conflicts in Business

Navigating the choppy waters of business invariably brings you face-to-face with conflicts, each as varied as the next. Understanding these variations is key to mastering the art of conflict resolution. Generally, conflicts in a business setting can be grouped into three main categories: relationship conflicts, task conflicts, and process conflicts.

Relationship conflicts emerge from interpersonal tensions. They often stem from miscommunications, personality clashes, or differing values. While seemingly petty, these conflicts can erode team cohesion and create a toxic work environment if left unchecked.

Task conflicts, on the other hand, arise from disagreements about the work itself. This could be a clash over the direction of a project, discrepancies in data interpretation, or differing views on how a task should be executed. Unlike relationship conflicts, task conflicts can sometimes be beneficial, as they encourage diversity of thought and can lead to better decision-making.

Process conflicts are all about the logistics – the who, how, when, and where of task completion. These conflicts often surface in scenarios where roles are undefined or where there is a perceived inequity in workload distribution. Like task conflicts, they can be constructive if managed correctly, encouraging more efficient processes and clearer roles.

Root Causes of Conflict

Peeling back the layers of any conflict often reveals its root causes – the underlying issues that need addressing for a lasting resolution. In business, these root causes typically include poor communication, unclear roles and responsibilities, power struggles, resource constraints, and differing personal values.

Poor communication is a frequent culprit. A message hurriedly conveyed can result in misunderstandings and speculations that spiral into conflicts. Ensuring that communication channels are open, clear, and used effectively is crucial.

Unclear roles and responsibilities can also lead to conflict. When team members aren't sure about what's expected of them, or if there's overlap between roles, frustration and conflict can ensue. Clearly defining everyone's role within the team is a straightforward remedy to this issue.

Power struggles often occur in environments where the leadership structure is not clear or is being challenged. This can create instability and uncertainty, fertile grounds for conflicts to thrive.

Resource constraints are another common trigger. When teams have to compete for limited resources, whether it's time, money, or manpower, tensions can quickly rise. Transparent and fair distribution systems can help mitigate these types of conflicts.

Lastly, differing personal values can lead to deep-seated conflicts. When core beliefs and values are challenged, or when there's a fundamental disagreement on ethical issues, resolution becomes complex and requires a sensitive approach.

Impact of Conflict on Performance

The impact of conflict on a business's performance can't be overstated. On the negative side, unresolved conflicts can lead to decreased productivity, poor teamwork, high stress levels, and ultimately, a high turnover rate. The constant friction can drain energy and divert focus from the actual objectives of the business, leading to missed opportunities and stunted growth.

However, not all conflict is detrimental. When handled correctly, conflict can have a positive impact on business performance. It can foster an environment where ideas are challenged and refined, leading to innovative solutions and better decision-making. It encourages resilience and adaptability among team members who learn how to handle disagreements constructively.

In your role as a business owner or entrepreneur, understanding the nature of conflicts, their roots, and their potential impacts on your business is pivotal. Recognizing that not all conflicts need to be doused but rather managed and sometimes even embraced can be a game changer. By adopting a strategic approach to conflict resolution, you can not only prevent potential disruptions but also enhance your team's creativity and cohesion, paving the way for a more resilient business model.

Remember, conflict in business is inevitable, but with the right tools and understanding, it can be managed effectively to promote growth and innovation.

Resolving Conflicts

Mediation Techniques

When the waters get choppy in the entrepreneurial sea, mediation serves as your lifeboat. It's a structured process where a neutral third party assists the disputants in reaching a consensus. It's not about imposing decisions, but facilitating a dialogue to uncover a mutually acceptable resolution.

Firstly, focus on creating the right environment. A neutral venue, where all parties feel safe, can set the stage for effective dialogue. This can be a quiet meeting room or a neutral off-site location. The key is to ensure that the setting does not confer power to any one party over another.

Begin the session by outlining the rules of engagement. These should include confidentiality agreements, speaking without interruptions, and respecting each person's point of view. Establishing these ground rules early on sets a tone of respect and cooperation.

Active listening is at the heart of successful mediation. Encourage each party to speak openly about their concerns without fear of judgement. As a mediator, your role is to listen attentively, summarise what's been said for clarity, and validate each party's feelings and perspectives. This helps to build empathy and often, empathy can lead to breakthroughs in conflict resolution.

Questioning techniques also play a critical role. Open-ended questions can help uncover underlying issues and lead to resolutions that are not apparent at first. For example, asking "What outcome would you consider fair?" can open up discussions that go beyond entrenched positions.

Finally, aim for win-win solutions. The ultimate goal of mediation isn't to declare a winner but to find a solution that all parties can live with moving forward. Encourage creative thinking about possible solutions, and how these can benefit all involved, rather than how they meet individual demands.

Conflict Resolution Styles

Understanding different conflict resolution styles can also empower you in handling business disputes more effectively. Everyone has a natural style, but flexibility is key in entrepreneurship.

The Thomas-Kilmann Conflict Mode Instrument (TKI) identifies five primary styles: Avoiding, Accommodating, Competing, Compromising, and Collaborating.

Avoiding is a low assertiveness, low cooperation approach where you simply sidestep the conflict. It's useful when the issue is trivial or when you need more time to think. However, use this sparingly; avoidance can often escalate the conflict if overused.

Accommodating involves playing down your own concerns to satisfy the other side, showing a high level of cooperation but low assertiveness. This can be effective when the relationship is more important than the conflict itself. Yet, be cautious, as overuse can lead to a loss of credibility and influence.

Competing is the opposite: high assertiveness and low cooperation. This is useful in quick, decisive leadership situations, like during emergencies. However, if used too frequently, it can breed resentment and deter open communication.

Compromising seeks to find a middle ground—a bit of give and take. This style is moderately assertive and cooperative, and it can lead to a quick resolution. However, it may not always be the most satisfying as neither party achieves what they fully want.

Collaborating is both highly assertive and cooperative. It involves digging into an issue to pinpoint the underlying needs and wants of both parties. This style is ideal for complex scenarios where you need to find an innovative solution that satisfies everyone. It requires time and effort but is often the most rewarding.

Each style has its place, and the key is to understand when to use each one effectively.

Strategies for De-escalation

De-escalation strategies are crucial in keeping a conflict from boiling over into an unmanageable situation. Begin by always maintaining your composure. Your ability to stay calm can have a calming effect on others, setting a tone that promotes constructive dialogue.

Use "I" statements to express concerns without casting blame. For example, say, "I feel frustrated when meetings start late" instead of "You're always late to meetings." This helps in keeping the discussion centered on solving issues rather than attacking personal traits.

Another effective technique is to agree before you disagree. Acknowledging valid points made by the other party before presenting your counterpoints can prevent them from becoming defensive. For instance, you might say, "I understand why you feel that way, and here's another perspective to consider."

Taking a timeout can also be beneficial. If emotions run high, pausing the discussion to allow everyone to cool down can prevent things from escalating. After a break, the parties can return more composed and ready to engage constructively.

Lastly, summarising what you've heard and understood can help to affirm that all parties are being heard. This not only ensures that you're on the same page but also demonstrates respect and appreciation for their input.

By integrating these mediation techniques, understanding the different conflict resolution styles, and employing de-escalation strategies, you can navigate through conflicts more effectively. Remember, the goal is not just to resolve the current issue but to strengthen the relationship for future collaboration.

Post-Conflict Management

Once the dust settles after a conflict, it's tempting to breathe a sigh of relief and move straight back to business as usual. However, savvy entrepreneurs know that the aftermath of a conflict, if handled with care, becomes a breeding ground for growth, innovation, and stronger relationships. This part of your journey is about turning past conflicts into future strengths.

Rebuilding Relationships

The immediate post-conflict phase is critical for relationship recovery. It's a time when trust is fragile, and every action you take can either repair or further damage your business relationships. Start by openly acknowledging the conflict and the issues it brought to the surface, rather than sweeping them under the rug. This transparency signals to all parties involved that you are serious about making changes and moving forward together.

Engage in active listening. This means giving your full attention to the other person when they are speaking, without planning your response while they talk. It shows respect and allows you to really understand their perspective. Remember, conflicts often arise from misunderstandings and miscommunications. By improving your listening skills, you're less likely to face similar issues in the future.

Next, invest time in understanding the emotional landscape of each team member involved in the conflict. Some might feel relieved that the issue is resolved, while others could be harbouring residual feelings of resentment or injustice. Address these emotions directly by having one-on-one conversations. This approach not only aids in healing but also bolsters individuals' commitment to the team and the common goals.

Furthermore, affirm each team member's value to the organization. Highlight their strengths and contributions, and assure them that their input is vital for the company's success. This can help to restore confidence and motivate team members to re-engage with the team dynamics positively.

Lastly, consider establishing new team rituals or traditions that can act as a reset button, reinforcing the new norms and the positive atmosphere you aim to cultivate. Whether it's a weekly team lunch, a monthly outing, or a regular team-building activity, these rituals can help forge stronger bonds and facilitate smoother collaboration.

Lessons Learned from Conflicts

Every conflict, regardless of its nature, comes with valuable lessons. As an entrepreneur, your ability to extract these lessons and use them to refine your business processes and communication strategies is crucial.

Start by conducting a post-mortem analysis of the conflict. What triggered it? How was it escalated? What worked or didn't work in the resolution process? Involve key team members in this reflection process to gain multiple perspectives and foster a culture of continuous improvement.

From this analysis, draw actionable insights. For instance, if the conflict arose from an unclear communication of job roles, consider reviewing and clarifying roles and responsibilities within your team. If decision-making bottlenecks contributed to the issue, it might be time to rethink your delegation processes or decision-making frameworks.

Document these insights in a shared space accessible to all team members, such as an internal wiki or a digital handbook. This not only helps in retaining organisational memory but also serves as a learning tool for existing and future team members.

Preventing Future Conflicts

While conflict is part and parcel of any entrepreneurial venture, there are strategies you can implement to reduce both the frequency and intensity of conflicts.

Firstly, set clear expectations right from the start. When everyone knows what's expected of them, there's less room for misinterpretations and frustrations. This includes clear communication about roles, responsibilities, and the company's goals.

Implement regular feedback mechanisms. This could be in the form of weekly check-ins, quarterly reviews, or real-time feedback tools. Such mechanisms ensure that minor grievances are aired and addressed promptly before they escalate into larger issues.

Invest in building a robust company culture that values open communication, respect, and collaboration. Culture can often be the first line of defence against conflict, creating an environment where differences are discussed openly and not allowed to fester.

Lastly, don't underestimate the power of training. Providing your team with training in communication, negotiation, and emotional intelligence can equip them with the skills to handle potential conflicts more effectively.

By focusing on these areas, you not only minimise the chances of conflicts reoccurring but also enhance your team's resilience and cohesion. Remember, effective post-conflict management is not just about damage control—it's about setting the stage for your next big success.

RECAP AND ACTION ITEMS

By now, you've dived deep into the dynamics of conflict in the business arena and explored various strategies to manage and resolve these inevitable clashes. Understanding the nature of conflict, deploying effective resolution techniques, and mastering the art of post-conflict management are critical skills that can significantly elevate your entrepreneurial journey.

Firstly, recognising the types of conflicts and their root causes is your initial step towards mastering conflict resolution. Whether these conflicts stem from miscommunication, personality clashes, or resource allocation, understanding their origins helps in addressing the underlying issues rather than just the symptoms. Take a moment to reflect on recent conflicts within your business. Can you identify the types? What were the root causes? Jot these down, as they will be invaluable in helping you foresee and possibly prevent future issues.

Moving on to resolving conflicts, remember that each situation is unique and demands a tailored approach. Techniques like mediation and understanding different conflict resolution styles can empower you and your team to handle disputes with finesse. Try role-playing a few conflict scenarios in your next team meeting. This exercise will not only enhance your team's mediation skills but also prepare you for real-life situations.

Lastly, the aftermath of a conflict, often overlooked, is crucial for maintaining a healthy work environment. Focus on rebuilding relationships and extracting lessons to refine your conflict management strategies continually. Implement a 'lessons learned' session following any significant conflict, discussing openly what went well and what didn't. This will not only help in healing the team but also in cementing stronger bonds moving forward.

Now, putting these insights into practice, create a conflict resolution handbook tailored to your business needs. Include signs to watch for, steps to mediate, and ways to ensure constructive post-conflict environments. This handbook can serve as a quick reference for you and your team, making conflict management more accessible and less daunting.

Remember, mastering conflict resolution can transform challenges into opportunities for growth and innovation. Embrace these strategies, refine them as you go, and watch your business culture and performance thrive.

BUILDING CHARISMA AND INFLUENCE

"Leadership is influence, nothing more, nothing less." - John C. Maxwell

The Charisma Factor

Charisma isn't just the reserve of celebrities or charismatic leaders; it's a magnetic quality that can be developed and honed, offering a significant advantage in the entrepreneurial world. Think of it as your silent partner in persuasion, opening doors and fostering connections that can propel your business forward.

Traits of Charismatic Leaders

Charisma is often perceived as an elusive trait, something you're either born with or not. However, this isn't entirely true. While some people may have a natural inclination towards charisma, the characteristics that make up this appealing quality can certainly be learned and cultivated.

First and foremost, charismatic leaders are typically very adept at communication. They know how to articulate their vision in a way that is clear, compelling, and infectious. But it's not just about talking; it's about engaging. These leaders listen actively, making those they interact with feel heard and valued, which in turn, enhances their likability.

Another key trait is confidence. This doesn't mean being overbearing or arrogant but possessing a quiet certainty about your abilities and decisions. This kind of confidence reassures others and draws them into your circle, making them feel secure in your leadership.

Empathy also plays a crucial role. Understanding and sharing the feelings of another person helps charismatic leaders connect on a deeper level, fostering strong bonds that can motivate and inspire teams.

Lastly, a sense of purpose and conviction often characterises these individuals. They know what they stand for and are passionate about their goals, which is contagious and can rally people to their cause.

Developing Personal Charisma

Now that we've outlined what makes a leader charismatic, you might be wondering how you can cultivate these traits within yourself. It's all about practice and mindset.

Start by enhancing your communication skills. Engage in active listening where you really focus on understanding the speaker, rather than just waiting for your turn to talk. This not only helps you gain insights but also shows respect, which boosts your likability.

Work on your confidence by setting and achieving small goals. This builds a track record of success that reinforces your self-esteem. Also, try to push yourself out of your comfort zones regularly; this can help diminish fears and build resilience, adding to your confidence.

Developing empathy can be as simple as making a conscious effort to imagine yourself in someone else's shoes. Try to understand their perspectives and emotions, especially in business settings where the stakes can be high, and emotions can run deep.

Lastly, refine your sense of purpose. Spend time reflecting on what you are passionate about and why you are pursuing your business goals. This clarity will not only help you make better decisions but will also enhance your ability to communicate your vision with conviction, a key aspect of charisma.

The Role of Authenticity

In the quest to be more charismatic, it's essential to remember the importance of authenticity. People have a keen radar for inauthentic behaviour, and nothing can undermine your charisma more than coming off as fake or insincere.

Authenticity starts with being true to yourself. Know your values, principles, and beliefs, and let these guide your actions and decisions. When your behaviour is a reflection of your inner self, you naturally become more consistent and reliable, traits that foster trust and respect.

Also, be transparent in your communications. If there are challenges or setbacks, don't shy away from sharing these with your team. Being open about difficulties as well as successes can enhance your credibility and humanise you, making your leadership more relatable and approachable.

In essence, the journey to increasing your charisma doesn't require you to transform into someone else. Rather, it's about enhancing and presenting the best version of yourself. By developing key traits like confident communication, empathy, and a clear sense of purpose, and by grounding these traits in authenticity, you can elevate your charismatic presence. This doesn't just make you a more effective leader; it makes you a magnetic one, capable of drawing in the right people and opportunities to succeed in the competitive world of entrepreneurship.

Influencing Others

Principles of Influence

Influence is a subtle art, especially in the entrepreneurial world where it can often mean the difference between success and failure. One of the foremost models to consider is Robert Cialdini's six principles of persuasion: reciprocity, commitment and consistency, social proof, authority, liking, and scarcity.

Reciprocity is about giving something to get something in return. As an entrepreneur, when you offer value first—be it through free resources, helpful advice, or genuine support—people are naturally inclined to return the favour. Think of it as planting seeds for future harvest.

Commitment and consistency are based on the principle that people like to act in harmony with their previous decisions and actions. Once someone commits, even in a small way, they are more likely to continue in a consistent manner. For instance, if your contacts agree to subscribe to your newsletter, they're more likely to engage with other content you offer.

Social proof is immensely powerful; it's the idea that individuals look to the behaviour and actions of others to determine their own. If you can show that other respected businesses or entrepreneurs endorse your product or service, new clients are more likely to consider you credible and trustworthy.

Authority suggests that people follow the lead of credible, knowledgeable experts. Publishing insightful articles, speaking at industry conferences, or gaining endorsements from recognised figures can increase your influence significantly.

Liking—people are easily persuaded by people they like. Building genuine connections, finding common interests, and demonstrating empathy can make you more relatable and influential.

Lastly, scarcity. It's about highlighting the uniqueness and limited availability of an opportunity. When used correctly, it creates a sense of urgency that can drive decision-making.

Influence without Authority

As an entrepreneur, you often need to influence stakeholders without having any formal authority over them. This could be when dealing with potential investors, partners, or even early customers. The key here is to leverage the power of persuasion and interpersonal skills.

First, understand the needs and desires of those you wish to influence. What drives them? What are their goals? Tailoring your approach based on these insights can significantly increase your influence.

Building a rapport is also crucial. People are more likely to be influenced by someone they trust and respect. Invest time in developing relationships before you need to influence. Listen actively, show empathy, and be responsive to their needs and concerns.

Another effective strategy is to demonstrate your value. How can your relationship be mutually beneficial? Be clear about what you bring to the table and how it aligns with their objectives. This could be through offering insights, sharing resources, or facilitating connections that benefit them.

Consistency in your interactions builds credibility. Be reliable and follow through on commitments. This consistency in character and action not only builds trust but also establishes your reputation as someone who is dependable and principled.

Lastly, use the principle of reciprocity. If you can help someone else before asking for anything, you establish a positive precedent for your interactions. This might mean making introductions, offering expert advice, or providing resources that can help them achieve their goals.

Ethical Considerations in Influence

Influencing others comes with a significant responsibility to act ethically. The line between influence and manipulation can sometimes become blurred. As a leader in your field, maintaining ethical integrity is not just important; it's essential for long-term success.

Transparency is key. Be clear about your intentions and the reasons behind your decisions. This prevents misunderstandings and builds trust. For example, if you are promoting a product, be upfront about its benefits and limitations.

Respect autonomy. While you may be influencing someone to make a decision that benefits your business, they should always feel free to make their own choices. Influence should be about guidance and persuasion, not coercion.

Consider the impact of your influence. Are your actions benefiting both parties? Are they fair and just? Long-term relationships are built on mutual benefits and respect. If your influence strategies are one-sided, they're likely unsustainable.

Be wary of overusing influence tactics like scarcity or authority, as they can easily lead to feelings of resentment or distrust if perceived as manipulative. Always balance these tactics with genuine value and respect for the other party's needs and wishes.

In conclusion, influencing others as an entrepreneur isn't just about getting what you want. It's about fostering respect, building genuine relationships, and acting with integrity. Whether you're dealing with a customer, a partner, or a competitor, how you influence today shapes your business landscape tomorrow.

Maintaining Influence

In the dynamic world of entrepreneurship, where every connection could lead to a new opportunity, maintaining influence is not just beneficial; it's essential. Let's dive into how you can sustain long-term relationships, manage influence within diverse teams, and adapt your influence strategies to remain effective and respected in your industry.

Sustaining Long-Term Relationships

You know how it goes. You meet someone, there's a spark of mutual interest, and you both see the potential for beneficial synergy. But as time ticks on, the initial excitement can fade, replaced by the humdrum of routine interaction. How do you keep these relationships not only alive but thriving?

Firstly, consider the power of consistent value. Always ask yourself, "What can I bring to this relationship that adds genuine value?" It might be insights from your industry, introductions to other key contacts, or even something as simple as a relevant article or book recommendation. By ensuring that each interaction leaves the other party better off, you solidify your position as a valuable contact worth keeping around.

Next, communication is your golden ticket. Regular check-ins, whether through email updates, quick calls, or coffee meetings, help keep the relationship active. However, the key here is relevance and respect for the other's time. Make these interactions meaningful rather than obligatory, focusing on quality over quantity.

Lastly, celebrate their successes as if they were your own. Send a quick congratulatory message when they hit a milestone, or better yet, share their achievements within your network. This not only strengthens the relationship but also reinforces your role as a supportive ally.

Influence in Diverse Teams

Diversity in teams brings a mixture of perspectives, which is a fertile ground for innovation but also a potential minefield for conflict. As an entrepreneur, your challenge is to harness this diversity and steer it towards a common goal.

Start with inclusion. Make it a point to understand and acknowledge the different backgrounds and viewpoints within your team. This could mean adapting your communication style to ensure everyone is on the same page or creating opportunities for each team member to contribute their unique insights.

Empathy plays a crucial role here. By showing genuine interest and effort to understand the individual experiences of team members, you build trust. And trust, as you well know, is the cornerstone of effective influence.

Furthermore, establish a culture of mutual respect and recognition. When team members feel valued, their commitment to the team's objectives strengthens. Facilitate this by setting clear expectations from the onset about the importance of respect and by leading by example.

Adapting Influence Strategies

The landscape of business is ever-changing, influenced by technological advancements, market shifts, and cultural trends. To maintain influence, you must be adaptable, ready to tweak your strategies in response to these changes.

Stay educated. Keep yourself updated with the latest in your industry and beyond. This doesn't mean jumping on every trend but having a solid understanding of how certain changes could impact your business and relationships.

Flexibility is your friend. What worked yesterday might not work today. For instance, if your traditional face-to-face networking events are losing steam, consider digital networking platforms or co-hosting webinars with industry peers. The method may change, but the goal of building and maintaining connections remains.

Experiment and measure. Don't shy away from trying new approaches to influence. Maybe a less formal, more conversational tone in your communications will resonate better with your digital-savvy stakeholders. Whatever adjustments you make, ensure you have metrics in place to evaluate their effectiveness. This data-driven approach allows you to refine your strategies continually.

In conclusion, maintaining influence in the entrepreneurial realm requires a blend of consistency, adaptability, and a deep understanding of the human element in business relationships. By focusing on providing value, embracing diversity, and being willing to adapt your strategies as needed, you ensure that your influence not only persists but grows.

RECAP AND ACTION ITEMS

Now that you've delved into the essentials of building charisma and influence, it's time to integrate what you've learnt into your daily entrepreneurial practice. Remember, the journey to becoming a charismatic leader and a persuasive influencer isn't about instant gratification. It's a continuous process of growth, authenticity, and ethical strategy.

Firstly, reflect on the traits of charismatic leaders you admire and pinpoint which of these traits you already possess and which you need to develop. Perhaps you are naturally confident but could work on your empathy. Start by setting small, daily goals to enhance these traits. For example, try to engage more deeply in your conversations today, listening actively and showing genuine interest.

Secondly, influencing others isn't just about having authority; it's about earning respect and trust. Begin by applying the principles of influence in your interactions without leaning on your position. Can you persuade a team member or a partner based on the strength of your argument or the passion of your vision rather than your role? Practice this. It could be as simple as pitching a new idea to your team and inviting open dialogue without pulling rank.

Ethical considerations are paramount. Always question your motives and the impact of your influence. Are you aiming for a win-win situation, or are you pushing for a personal agenda? Keep ethics at the core of your influence to build lasting respect and integrity.

For sustaining long-term relationships, make a conscious effort to appreciate the diverse perspectives within your team. This could involve monthly feedback sessions where you not only offer insight but actively solicit it, showing that you value everyone's input.

Lastly, the world and its markets are ever-changing, and so should your strategies of influence. Stay adaptable. Perhaps once a quarter, take time to review your influencing techniques and their effectiveness. Adjust as necessary, embracing new ideas and technologies that can enhance your communication and leadership.

By consistently applying these strategies, you will not only enhance your charisma and influence but also lead your ventures with greater impact and success. Remember, the power of influence is most effective when combined with genuine intent and ethical action. Keep these principles in mind, and you're all set to elevate your entrepreneurial journey.

CONTINUOUS IMPROVEMENT IN COMMUNICATION

"The only impossible journey is the one you never begin." - Tony Robbins

Self-Assessment and Reflection

Dive deep into the realm of self-assessment and reflection, where the path to mastering the art of communication begins with a good look in the mirror. As an entrepreneur, your ability to convey your vision, negotiate deals, and inspire your team hinges on continuous self-improvement. Let's break down how you can harness self-assessment tools, learn from past communication faux pas, and set impactful personal development goals.

Tools for Self-Assessment

The journey of enhancing your communicative prowess starts with knowing where you stand. It's a bit like stepping on a scale - it might not always show what you want, but it provides the essential starting point for improvement. Here are a few tools that can help you gauge your current communication skills:

1. **360-Degree Feedback:** This is not just feedback from your peers but also from subordinates, supervisors, and sometimes, even clients. It offers a panoramic view of how your communication is perceived across the board. It's like getting a mirror that reflects not just your face but your entire surroundings. Tools like Officevibe or SurveyMonkey can help you gather this type of feedback efficiently.

2. **Self-Recording:** In the age of smartphones, this tool is as accessible as it is effective. Record your presentations or meetings (with consent, of course) and play them back to observe your verbal and non-verbal cues. Are you speaking too quickly? Do your hands flail about as if directing traffic? Observing yourself

can be an eye-opener and guide you on what to tweak.

3. **Personality Assessments:** Tools like the Myers-Briggs Type Indicator or the DISC assessment can provide insights into your communication style and how it meshes or clashes with others. Understanding whether you're an ENTJ or an ISFP, for example, can shed light on how your inherent traits influence your communication strengths and challenges.

Reflecting on Communication Failures

Now, onto a less comfortable but incredibly valuable part—reflecting on when things didn't go quite right. Every entrepreneur has stories of mishaps and miscommunications. The key isn't to dwell on these as failures but to view them as rich, albeit painful, learning opportunities.

1. **Case Study Yourself:** Think back to a recent situation where the outcome was not what you expected—perhaps a pitch that went south or a team meeting that ended in confusion rather than clarity. Document what happened, what was said, how it was interpreted, and the aftermath. Identifying the disconnect can often illuminate what needs to change next time.

2. **Seek Out Feedback:** After a less-than-successful communication, follow up with those involved and ask for their perspective on what went wrong. This might be uncomfortable, but true growth often lies on the other side of comfort. Ensure you approach this as a learning exercise, not a blame game.

3. **Reflect Regularly:** Make this a regular practice rather than a once-in-a-blue-moon post-mortem. Set aside time each week to review your communications. This could be 30 minutes at the end of the week where you reflect on one or two key conversations and jot down notes on what went well and what could have been better.

Setting Personal Development Goals

With a clear understanding of your current abilities and past pitfalls, you're now primed to set personal development goals that are both challenging and achievable. Communication is a vast arena, ranging from public speaking and negotiation to emotional intelligence and active listening. Here's how to set goals that resonate:

1. **Be S.M.A.R.T About It:** The S.M.A.R.T (Specific, Measurable, Achievable, Relevant, Time-bound) framework isn't just corporate jargon; it's an effective tool that can crystallise your goals into actionable steps. For instance, instead of vaguely aiming to "improve public speaking skills," set a goal to "attend a public speaking workshop by Q3 and deliver at least two presentations to the team each month."

2. **Focus on Strengths and Weaknesses:** While it's crucial to bolster your weak spots, it's equally important to capitalize on your strengths. If you're great at explaining complex ideas but poor at non-verbal cues, set goals for each area to ensure balanced growth.

3. **Commit to Learning:** Set goals that involve learning new skills or enhancing existing ones. This could be through books, online courses, or workshops. For instance, if you've identified a need to improve your negotiation skills, you might set a goal to read "Never Split the Difference" by Chris Voss and then apply one tactic from the book each week during negotiations.

As you delve into these practices of self-assessment, reflection, and goal setting, remember that the path to becoming an exceptional communicator is not a sprint but a marathon. Each step you take to reflect on your interactions, understand your communication style, and set targeted goals paves the way to not just becoming a better leader or entrepreneur but a truly impactful communicator.

Professional Development in Communication

Training and Workshops

In the fast-paced world of entrepreneurship, staying ahead requires not just keeping your skills sharp, but continuously honing them. Training and workshops are not just checkboxes on professional development plans; they are your strategic tools for mastering communication. Whether it's a local seminar or an international conference, each session is a potential goldmine for enhancing your communication arsenal.

Consider workshops as your personal lab where you can experiment with new communication strategies and tools under the guidance of experts. These controlled environments allow you to explore complex scenarios and receive feedback in real-time, which is invaluable. It's like having a safety net while you're practising high-wire tricks of rhetoric and persuasion.

Moreover, training sessions are tailored to diverse levels of expertise and areas of focus, from negotiation skills to digital communication platforms. As an entrepreneur, your aim should be to identify workshops that not just align with your current business needs but also push the envelope, encouraging you to think and communicate in innovative ways. For instance, a workshop on storytelling could revolutionise the way you pitch to investors, turning your presentations from informative to compelling.

Always approach these learning opportunities with a clear goal. Before attending any workshop, ask yourself what the takeaways should be and how they will apply to your specific business scenarios. Post-workshop, it's crucial to integrate these learnings into your daily communications, be it through emails, presentations, or your marketing materials.

Mentorship and Coaching

While workshops equip you with the tools, mentorship and coaching embed these tools through tailored guidance and sustained support. Having a mentor is like having a GPS in the world of communication – they help you navigate, recalibrate and reach your destination more efficiently.

Finding the right mentor, someone who embodies where you want to be in terms of communication prowess, can catapult your skills from adequate to exceptional. This relationship offers a mix of professional wisdom, personal anecdotes, and corrective feedback that is hard to find in formal educational settings.

Coaching, on the other hand, often involves a more structured approach to developing specific communication skills. A coach can work with you to dissect your communication events, such as important pitches or team meetings, and provide actionable feedback on areas of improvement. They can also role-play various business scenarios with you to foster a practical understanding of effective communication strategies.

When selecting a mentor or a coach, look for someone who not only speaks well but listens effectively too. Effective communication is as much about listening and understanding as it is about speaking, and a good mentor or coach will model this balance. They should challenge you, not just cheer you on, pushing you out of your comfort zones and helping you grow.

Keeping up with Communication Trends

The landscape of communication is continuously evolving. What worked yesterday might not yield the same results today. Therefore, keeping abreast of the latest trends is crucial. This doesn't mean chasing every new buzzword or tool. Rather, it's about discerning which emerging trends can beneficially impact your business communication strategies.

Social media platforms, for example, have transformed traditional business communications, creating direct lines to customers but also new challenges in managing brand voice and online interactions. Staying updated on the best practices for these platforms can dramatically improve how you engage with your audience.

Furthermore, advancements in communication technology such as AI-driven analytics for customer interaction and automated CRM systems are reshaping how businesses understand and cater to their clients. By staying informed about these technologies, you can adopt early and integrate them into your communication strategy to streamline processes and enhance efficiency.

Professional publications, podcasts, and industry newsletters are great resources for keeping your finger on the pulse of communication trends. Dedicate time each week to explore these materials and think critically about how you can apply what you learn to your business.

Through training and workshops, mentorship and coaching, and staying updated with the latest trends, you can ensure that your communication skills grow in tandem with your business. Remember, in the realm of entrepreneurship, effective communication is not just about sharing information; it's about inspiring action, building relationships, and driving innovation.

Future Trends in Communication

Technological Advancements

As you navigate the ever-evolving landscape of business communication, it's crucial to stay ahead of the curve with the latest technological advancements. The digital age continues to unfold with groundbreaking innovations that significantly impact how we communicate.

One key development you should be aware of is the rise of AI-driven communication tools. These platforms use artificial intelligence to enhance interactions by providing real-time language translation, sentiment analysis, and personalised communication strategies. For example, imagine AI tools that analyse the tone and style of your emails, suggesting adjustments to improve clarity and impact based on the recipient's communication preferences and past interactions.

Another technological leap is the integration of augmented reality (AR) and virtual reality (VR) in communication practices. These technologies are transforming remote interactions, making them more immersive and effective. For instance, VR meetings can simulate a real-life conference environment, allowing participants to feel as if they are in the same room, which can greatly enhance the connection and engagement levels during remote pitches or negotiations.

Blockchain technology also offers significant advantages, particularly in terms of security and transparency in business communications. Utilising blockchain can help ensure that every transaction and communication is recorded in a verifiable and unalterable way, which is particularly beneficial in industries where confidentiality and data integrity are paramount.

To integrate these technologies effectively, consider partnering with tech startups or investing in training sessions that focus on digital tools and platforms. Keeping abreast of these advancements not only enhances your communication capabilities but also offers a competitive edge in an increasingly digital marketplace.

The Evolving Landscape of Business Communication

The landscape of business communication is shifting more rapidly than ever before, influenced by globalisation, changing workforce demographics, and cultural shifts. Understanding these changes is crucial for maintaining relevance and effectiveness in your communication strategies.

Globalisation has expanded the marketplace beyond local and national borders, necessitating the ability to communicate across cultures and languages. As an entrepreneur, you need to cultivate a global mindset, which includes understanding cultural nuances and adapting your communication style accordingly. This might mean learning to convey respect and clarity in cultures where indirect communication is the norm, or becoming adept at managing virtual teams across different time zones.

The demographic changes in the workforce, particularly with the rise of Millennials and Gen Z, are also reshaping business communication. These younger generations prefer transparency, instant communication, and value-driven narratives. Tools like instant messaging apps, social media platforms, and video content are becoming indispensable. Moreover, these generations often champion ethical practices and sustainability, which should be reflected in your company's communication, be it internal or external.

Lastly, the increasing focus on mental health and well-being in the workplace is changing how businesses communicate. It's becoming imperative to adopt a more empathetic and supportive tone, ensuring that communications are not only informative but also considerate of employees' mental health.

To navigate this evolving landscape, continually assess and adapt your communication strategies to align with these broader cultural and demographic shifts. This might involve regular training sessions focused on cultural competence or updating internal communication policies to include new digital communication platforms.

Preparing for Future Communication Challenges

As you look to the future, it's not just about adopting new technologies or understanding global trends; it's also about anticipating and preparing for potential communication challenges.

One significant challenge is information overload. In an age where data is abundant, the ability to sift through the noise and present clear, concise, and relevant information is more critical than ever. To tackle this, develop strategies for effective information management and prioritisation. Tools like AI-driven data analysis can help identify key messages and trends that need your attention.

Another upcoming challenge is the increasing importance of crisis communication. In today's fast-paced and often unpredictable business environment, the ability to communicate effectively during a crisis can make or break your reputation. Prepare by establishing a comprehensive crisis communication plan that includes predefined communication channels, key messages, and protocols for different scenarios. Regularly training your team in these procedures ensures everyone is ready to respond swiftly and appropriately.

Lastly, consider the ethical implications of your communication strategies. As privacy concerns and regulations like GDPR (General Data Protection Regulation) become more prominent, ensuring that your communication practices are not only effective but also compliant and ethical is essential. This might involve more stringent data handling procedures or clearer communication with customers about how their information is used.

By staying informed about these potential challenges and preparing accordingly, you can ensure that your business communication remains robust and responsive to the demands of the modern world.

RECAP AND ACTION ITEMS

By now, you've equipped yourself with powerful tools and insights to elevate your communication skills. The journey of continuous improvement in communication isn't a one-time task but an ongoing process that can significantly impact your success as an entrepreneur.

CONTINUOUS IMPROVEMENT IN COMMUNICATION

Firstly, take the insights from your self-assessment tools and reflect deeply on where your communication has faltered. This isn't just about recognising errors but understanding the nuances that could transform your future interactions. Set clear, measurable personal development goals. Perhaps you want to increase your public speaking engagements or improve your email etiquette. Whatever it is, write it down, make it specific, and set deadlines.

Moving on to professional development, if you haven't already, enrol in training sessions or workshops that focus on areas you're looking to strengthen. These could range from negotiation skills to effective storytelling. Remember, the investment you make in improving your communication skills can provide exponential returns in the form of better relationships and more closed deals.

Additionally, consider finding a mentor or coach who excels in communication. The right mentor can provide not only guidance but also feedback that helps you see blind spots in your communication style. Keep your eyes peeled for new trends and tools that emerge—staying updated is key in this rapidly changing world.

As for the future trends, stay curious and adaptable. The way we communicate is evolving, driven by technological advancements and changing business landscapes. Prepare yourself to embrace new communication platforms and styles. Understanding these can help you not only keep up but stand out in your business practices.

Your action steps? Identify one area from each section we've discussed that you feel needs the most improvement. Allocate time weekly to focus on these areas, whether it's reflecting on past communication failures, attending a new workshop, or researching emerging communication technologies.

Remember, the art of communication is vast and varied. By continuously refining your skills, you're setting yourself—and your business—up for lasting success. Let's keep the conversation going and your entrepreneurial journey thriving.

EMBRACING YOUR COMMUNICATION JOURNEY

As you turn the pages of this insightful exploration into the facets of effective communication, you've embarked on a journey that transcends the mere act of reading. You've been equipped with a suite of tools, each chapter a stepping stone towards mastering the art of interaction in both personal and professional realms. Now, as we draw this exploration to a close, it's imperative to reflect not only on how far you've come but also on how you can continue to cultivate these skills in every facet of your life.

Effective communication is an art form, one that you have begun to master through understanding and practice. It is the cornerstone of leadership, the heartbeat of relationships, and the scaffold upon which your professional interactions are built. As you have learnt, mastering the art of listening opens the door to truly understanding those around you, while the power of your voice allows you to influence and inspire.

Non-verbal communication cues have shown you that what remains unsaid can often speak volumes, and crafting compelling messages ensures your voice is not just heard but remembered. Digital communication dynamics have highlighted the modern challenges and solutions in our interconnected world. Each subsequent chapter has built upon this foundation, guiding you towards becoming not just a communicator but a connoisseur of connection.

The essence of communication is transformation. It transforms relationships, perspectives, and even outcomes in business and personal interactions. The skills you've honed will set you apart in a world where many hear, but few truly listen. In every conversation, you now have the opportunity to create meaningful impact, to be the leader who inspires action and fosters an environment of openness and growth.

However, the journey does not end here. The landscape of communication is ever-evolving, and so too should your strategies and approaches. This book has provided you with the initial tools and concepts, but the continuation of this journey is just as critical as its commencement.

Now, consider the future. Imagine a scenario where your communication skills could not only improve but become pivotal in defining your career trajectory or personal relationships. Where do you see yourself if you continue to develop these skills? Leading with greater empathy, negotiating with unmatched prowess, or perhaps inspiring change in your community or organisation? The possibilities are boundless.

But achieving this does not come from complacency; it requires continuous effort, reflection, and adaptation. Always seek out new learning opportunities, be open to feedback, and remember that every interaction is a chance to practise and refine your skills. Look for moments to apply the subtle art of non-verbal cues, the assertiveness of your voice, and the strategic crafting of your messages.

Should you find yourself in need of further guidance, seeking a deeper understanding of advanced communication strategies, or simply wishing to explore tailored advice specific to your unique challenges, do not hesitate to reach out. Connect with Neil and Ian on LinkedIn to discover how professional guidance can elevate your mastery of communication to new heights. Together, we can ensure that your communication skills continue to grow, adapt, and inspire, no matter the context.

In closing, remember that the art of communication is about more than just exchanging information. It's about understanding the emotion and intentions behind the information. It's about how you share yourself with the world and how you allow others to share themselves with you. It's about connecting, influencing, and leading in ways that enrich and enhance your life and the lives of others.

As you move forward, keep in mind that every word you speak, every message you craft, and every feedback you consider has the potential to foster understanding, build relationships, and create opportunities. With the tools you now possess, you are well on your way to becoming not just a participant in conversations but a creator of connections.

Embrace this journey with enthusiasm and confidence, knowing that with each word, you are weaving the fabric of your legacy in the tapestry of human interaction.

Let the dialogue continue, and may your communications always be impactful.

www.ingramcontent.com/pod-product-compliance
Lightning Source LLC
Chambersburg PA
CBHW050310230526
45471CB00005B/2110